Be Kind to Your Mother (Earth)

An Original Play

Be Kind to Your Mother (Earth)

An Original Play

by Douglas Love

HarperCollins*Publishers*

1 2 3 4 5 6 7 8 9 10

First Edition

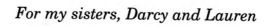

For my sisters, Darcy and Lauren

Introduction

The first time I stepped inside a theater, I thought that it was the most magical place in the world. I went with my class to see a show at the performing arts center in my town. It was a musical for children produced by a professional company of actors. I was immediately captivated. Right there in front of me, performers were singing and dancing and telling a story—live! It seemed that they were talking directly to me, and I was completely enthralled with the characters and their adventures. The sets and costumes weren't fancy or extravagant, but this made me even more involved in the production. I had to use my imagination to pick up where the limitations of the sets and costumes left off. This first production was my introduction to the world of the theater.

You are about to embark on an exciting adventure. Planning, rehearsing, and staging a play can be a fun and satisfying experience. It's up to you to make your play the best it can be. The written script is only the beginning. It is meant to be used like a map, a route that guides you through the story.

Because actors in a play are right in front of an audience (not up on a movie screen or inside a television), anything can happen, and it usually does. Scenery may fall over, people may say the wrong lines at the wrong time or forget their lines altogether. When these mistakes happen, the actors can't stop and start over. In the theater, they go right on and try to get back on track with as much ease as possible. This is the challenge of live theater. The feeling that *anything can happen* keeps everyone on their toes.

While working on your production, don't be discouraged if you feel that you don't have the exact prop or costume that the play calls for. If the stage directions call for a couch in a certain scene, there is no rule that says you can't use a bench, or a chair, or nothing at all instead. You decide what you think is important to include. Some of the best plays have no props or stage settings at all. The audience has to use its imagination, which can be a lot of fun.

It is almost always helpful to have someone serve as the director of the play, whether you are performing in your school or your backyard. This person will help make decisions about the direction your production takes: Will everyone wear costumes? Will you make a set? Who will play which character? He or she may also designate certain parts of the stage to be different places where the action takes place. The director should also help everyone working on the play realize that theater is a collaborative art. This means that the talents of a lot of people come together to create one exciting production that everyone can be proud of because everyone helped to create it.

Performers have a special task in the play. When you know what role you will play, the next step is to develop your character. This is achieved by asking yourself a lot of questions: If I was this person (or animal), how would I walk? How would I stand? How would I speak? What would I wear? Whom do I like in the play? Whom don't I like? What do I want to do in the play? You can and should ask yourself these and more questions about your character. Then, you have to answer these questions and make some decisions. If you are playing an old man, you might decide to stand hunched over and walk with a cane. You may choose to have a gravelly voice and tattered clothes. You may discover while reading the play that you are a rich old man who doesn't spend any of his money, and you are afraid that everyone is trying to steal it.

The answers and decisions that you make

about your character are guideposts on your journey. It's okay to change your mind if something isn't working. None of the choices that you make for your character are wrong. Experiment! That's what rehearsals are for.

Rehearsal is extremely important if you plan to perform your play for an audience. Some theater directors and actors believe that you should rehearse one hour for every minute that you are onstage. Some of that rehearsal time can be spent on your own, memorizing your lines. Different people memorize lines differently, but all techniques have one thing in common—repetition. Go over and over and over your lines until you can say them without looking at the script. Some people sit alone reading their lines again and again until they can say them from memory. Others read their lines into a tape recorder and listen to the tape over and over. Or ask a friend or someone in your family to "hold book." This means that he reads the line that comes before yours and then you say your line.

Rehearsal is also the time to decide on your blocking, or the physical action of the play. Who does what, when? If everything is planned before the performance, you'll feel more secure, and the audience will be able to follow the story more easily.

When planning your blocking, remember that

you are performing for an audience that needs to see what is going on to follow the story of the play. Important action should take place closer to the audience. Try to face the audience as much as possible; this allows them to see your facial expressions and hear you better.

Whether you will be performing on your school stage, in your classroom, or at home, feel free to make changes to make the play work for you.

About *Be Kind to Your Mother (Earth)*

What if you could travel back in time to fix a problem? Wouldn't that be great? You could change things in the past and then return to the present. Everything that went wrong would be right.

This is the idea behind *Be Kind to Your Mother (Earth)*. Three friends decide that the pollution on Earth is so bad that they will travel back in time to try to stop pollution from ever starting. But by the end of the play, Chester, Deedee, and Kato discover that the only way to fix the Earth's pollution problem is to work in the present to change the future.

The Characters

The following descriptions of the characters in *Be Kind to Your Mother (Earth)* are just a starting point. It is up to you to fully develop your own character by reading the play carefully, and forming your own opinion about your character's personality.

Grandma Jones and **Grandchild Jones** live in the year 2053. They are a lot like grandparents and grandchildren today. The grandchild doesn't want to go to bed and the grandma is worn out from her busy day.

Chester, Deedee, and **Kato** are three concerned kids who become fed up with their polluted environment and decide that they must do something about it.

Papa, Patty, and **Peewee Picnic** are a very sloppy family who do not care about pollution or littering.

Mother Nature is a magical creature who comes and goes. With her travel the fairylike **Children of the Atmosphere**. The children are sick because of the polluted state of the environment. Unfortunately, Mother Nature has no control over the actions of humans.

Benny is a used time machine salesman. He is a fast-talking wheeler-dealer.

Grandpa Garbage loves garbage. He is a bad guy who enjoys and helps create pollution.

The **Boston Tea Party Colonists** are very surprised to see Chester, DeeDee, and Kato suddenly appear at the docks. They think that the children are magical spirits.

George Washington, the first president of the United States, is a young boy when we meet him in this play. His mother makes him pick cherries from a tree in his backyard and he is not happy about it.

George's mom is a good-natured woman who just wants her son to finish his chores.

The **Dodo Birdies** are silly birds who are looking for the youngest of their flock. They aren't particularly intelligent.

Sets and Props

As you read through the play, a picture will form in your mind of how a certain scene looks. Think about this picture and how you can recreate it onstage with sets and props. The goal of sets and props is to give an audience a feeling of where the action is taking place.

The first scene in this play takes place in the year 2053! You decide what things should look like. Of course no one knows how the world will really look then, so you can't make mistakes! The walls might be silver or gold. Or maybe the future will have computer screens all over the place.

The pond in Scene 2 can look like a park or a backyard. There might be a bench or a picnic table. The Picnic family should carry a large basket of food. Grandpa Garbage should have garbage sticking out of all his pockets. He can throw it around throughout the play, always leaving a trail of garbage. There is garbage everywhere! Empty boxes, milk containers, and egg cartons are fun to use.

The time machine can be made out of an old box or a big piece of cardboard that the actors can hold in front of them. Decorate it so it looks like it has the power to travel through time.

For the Boston Tea Party in Scene 3 you might write "Tea" on some large boxes in big block letters. Try to find ropes, sails, and anything else that you think might be found on a dock. In Scene 4, George Washington needs a cherry tree. You can make this out of paper and markers, use a real fallen branch, or have an actor (with a green outfit and leaves attached to him) portray the tree. George Washington's mother gives him a basket to collect cherries from the tree. You can use the picnic basket from Scene 2. You also need three trees for the Dodo birds in Scene 5.

Keep in mind that the changing of scenes shouldn't stop the action of the play for too long. Once you have an audience interested in your story, keep them interested! Long scene changes can be boring so make sure you practice these as well as your lines.

Costumes

Be *Kind to Your Mother (Earth)* has some characters who could wear what kids wear today. Others need your imagination to create a look that you think will help the audience understand the story more clearly. Remember, these are only suggestions. Feel free to use your imagination to create costumes from materials that are easily available to you.

Grandma Jones and **Grandchild Jones** exist in the future. What can they wear to show us that they are from a time that hasn't happened yet? What do you think we'll be wearing in 2053?

Chester, DeeDee, and **Kato** are regular kids from the present day. They can be wearing everyday street clothes.

Papa, Patty, and **PeeWee Picnic** are all

litterbugs so they may dress sloppily. They are also from the present day.

Mother Nature and the **Children of the Atmosphere** should look magical and very natural. Perhaps they could have leaves, branches, or flowers attached to green clothes.

Benny might wear loud, colorful clothes with lots of watches on his wrists and ankles, or hanging inside an overcoat.

Grandpa Garbage should look like his name. He might wear a necklace of egg cartons and old cereal boxes or a hat covered with crumpled paper and old cans.

The **Colonists, George Washington**, and **George's mom** should look like people who lived during the late 1700s, during the American Revolution. The women wore long, dark dresses and the men often wore knickers, ruffled shirts, and knee socks. Check the encyclopedia or ask a teacher for more information.

The **Dodo Birdies** should be dressed very colorfully, and all look the same. They could all wear shorts or leotards or orange vests and hats. They might wear wings made out of paper and attached with string. It's up to you!

Cast

In the year 2053:
Grandma Jones
Grandchild Jones

In the year 1993:
Chester
DeeDee
Kato
Papa Picnic
Patty Picnic
PeeWee Picnic
Mother Nature
The Children of the Atmosphere
  (minimum of 3 actors)
Benny, the used time machine salesman
Grandpa Garbage, the villain!

The Boston Tea Party, 1771:
The colonists: Marnie, Tom, Jean, Pete, Sam,
  Jessica

At Mount Vernon, 1738:
George Washington
  (as a boy with a cherry tree)
George's mom

Dodo Island, 1500s:
The Dodo Birdies: Dotty, Dingy, Dizzy, Daffy, Mama Dodo, Baby Dodo

Optional Smaller Cast—11 actors

Actor 1: Chester
Actor 2: DeeDee
Actor 3: Kato
Actor 4: Grandpa Garbage
Actor 5: Grandma Jones, Marnie, Dotty
Actor 6: Grandchild Jones, Child of the Atmosphere, Dingy, Jessica
Actor 7: Papa Picnic, Tom, George Washington, Dizzy
Actor 8: Patty Picnic, Child of the Atmosphere, Jean, Mama Dodo
Actor 9: PeeWee Picnic, Child of the Atmosphere, Pete
Actor 10: Mother Nature, George's Mom, Daffy
Actor 11: Benny, Sam, Baby Dodo

★ *The above is only a suggestion and can be done with even fewer actors by cutting some of the Dodos and colonists.*

★ *For more parts you can add more Children of the Atmosphere.*

Setting

Scene 1

★ *Time: Year 2053*

★ *GRANDMA JONES is getting GRANDCHILD JONES ready for bed. There is one single bed stage left. Just right of the bed is a rocking chair. There is a window upstage right that can open and close.*

Grandchild: Grandma, I don't want to go to bed yet. I'm not tired! Let me stay up and de-moleculize something.

Grandma: You're not tired? You've been running around here all day! Not only that, we went to the planetarium and the jet propulsion center and we toured the meteorite! I'm worn out!

Grandchild: I'm not! I want to hear a story!

Grandma: A story! Goldilocks and the Three Androids? Or Little Red Shooting Star?

Grandchild: That's kid's stuff! I want to hear a real story!

15

★ *At that moment, debris flies in the window. It is pollution.*

Grandma: Oh, dear! *(She crosses to shut the window.)* The pollution level is so high today!

Grandchild: They finally plowed a path through the old park. Before that we couldn't even walk through it, there was so much garbage! It smelled really bad too! P.U.! Were things this polluted when you were a kid, Grandma?

Grandma: There was pollution. That's for sure. But not this bad. We used to be able to look out the window of a four-story building and see the ground when we looked down. Now all you see is smog, and if you could see the ground, you'd see that it's covered with garbage.

Grandchild: Why does the sun shine only twelve minutes a day?

Grandma: That's air pollution, dear. It's caused a haze all around the planet.

Grandchild: Yuck.

Grandma: Yuck is right. If we didn't have air purifying systems in our homes, we'd never breathe clean air. *(Thinking it over)* You want to hear a story? I've got a story for you. It's a true story too! When I was your age, back in 1993 . . .

Grandchild: 1993! Wow, you're old! Did they have dinosaurs back then?

Grandma: No, dear. Listen to Grandma's story. Back in 1993, I knew three kids who were very upset about the condition of the environment.

Grandchild: So there *was* pollution back in the dark ages.

★ *Lights dim.*

★ *The stage changes to represent a change in time. This can be achieved by the actors moving offstage in slow motion and the next group of actors moving onstage in slow motion. (There could also be signs that are flipped with the years printed on them. These signs could remain onstage and change each time the action of the play moves into another year.)*

★ *End of Scene*

Scene 2

★ *Time: Year 1993*

★ *Three kids, CHESTER, DEEDEE, and KATO, sit near a pond, relaxing. A group of kids on a picnic with GRANDPA GARBAGE and his son, PAPA, run on stage and start to pollute the entire area.*

Grandpa Garbage: Come on! Come on over here! I found a great spot for us to picnic!

Papa: Come on, kids! Patty! PeeWee! This way! Grandpa's found us a spot. *(He begins to stretch out a picnic blanket.)*

Patty: I don't like this spot! Yuck! You're not going to lay that blanket on the yuckie ground! In the dirt!

Papa: Ah! A little dirt never hurt anybody! Besides, I'm hungry! I didn't want to go on this picnic! It was all your grandpa's idea.

Grandpa Garbage: Come on, kids! We have some good food here! Here *(handing some sandwiches to*

18

PEEWEE), pass these out.

PeeWee: Goodie, goodie, goodie!

Patty: What should I do with the wrapper?

Papa: Just throw it in the water. It doesn't matter. Just look around. There's so much pollution, a few more wrappers aren't going to make any difference.

★ *They proceed to eat things and throw their garbage all over the stage.*

Patty: I'm done!

Papa: I'm done!

PeeWee: I'm done!

Grandpa Garbage: You all run along and play. I'll catch up to you.

★ *(PAPA, PATTY, and PEEWEE exit. GRANDPA GARBAGE hides in the corner and listens to CHESTER, DEEDEE, and KATO's conversation.)*

Chester: Did you see that? They just threw all of their garbage all over the place.

19

Kato: Some of it went into our pond!

DeeDee: Wait a minute! I think I've got something!

Kato: Pull it in!

★ *(DEEDEE has been fishing in the pond all this time. She reels in her catch. It is an old shoe.)*

Chester: That's it! I'm going to complain to someone!

Kato: To whom?

Chester: I don't know! To our congressperson!

Kato: We're just kids! They're not going to listen to us. We have to find someone with power! With experience! With the ability to get the job done!

DeeDee *(looking offstage)*: Someone's coming!

★ *(MOTHER NATURE enters with THE CHILDREN OF THE ATMOSPHERE.)*

Mother Nature: Children! Try to stay in line! Don't get lost! Here, here. Let's stop and rest a moment! Dip your tiny toes in the pond.

DeeDee: Who are you?

Mother Nature: Who are you!?

DeeDee: I asked you first.

Mother Nature: What does that have to do with the price of potatoes?

DeeDee: The price of what?

Mother Nature: Potatoes!

DeeDee: I don't know. What DOES it have to do with the price of potatoes?

Mother Nature: I asked you first.

DeeDee: I'm so confused!

Mother Nature: I was just fooling, dear! That was just an expression.

DeeDee: Oh, well, then I was just fooling too.

★ *There is a clap of thunder and some lightning.*

Mother Nature: It's not nice to fool Mother Nature!

21

DeeDee: I'm still confused!

Chester: You're Mother Nature? Wow! Am I glad that you came along. We need to talk! There is far too much littering and polluting going on around here!

Kato: Just look around! There is garbage everywhere! And this is from only one family!

Mother Nature: You don't have to tell me about pollution. Pollution has been around for centuries! I do fear that it will stick around for centuries more.

Chester: If it sticks around there won't be more centuries. Soon all the garbage will take over, and we'll all be in it up to our eyebrows!

Mother Nature: You can't change the past! People are used to littering! They don't understand that when they throw their trash on the ground or in the water, it hurts our environment. And they're cutting down trees, not to mention the number of endangered species there are now.

DeeDee: What can we do?

Mother Nature: I wish I knew. The condition of

the earth is making my Children of the
Atmosphere quite ill. Every time someone
throws garbage on the ground, or out their car
window or into our rivers, lakes, and oceans, my
Children of the Atmosphere get very, very sick.
*(THE CHILDREN OF THE ATMOSPHERE cough and
moan.)*

Mother Nature: Well, we must be running
along. This so-called fresh air isn't good for my
children.

★ *They exit.*

Kato: I don't get it. Why did people start littering
and cutting down trees?

Chester: You heard what Mother Nature said.
They're used to it. They've been doing it for
centuries.

Kato: If only we could go back and tell them not
to start!

DeeDee: We'd need some kind of time machine to
do that.

★ *Used time machine salesman* BENNY *enters
with a* boing!

Benny: Did someone say that they needed a time machine?

DeeDee: Who are you?

Benny: Benny! I sell time machines—new and used. I've also got watches. *(BENNY rolls up his jacket sleeve to show watches strapped all the way up his arm.)*

Kato: We need a time machine!

Benny: You're in luck. I got my last one—still available.

Chester: New or used?

Benny: Used—but only by a little old lady who used to take it to the seventeenth century on Sundays.

Kato: How much?

★ *(BENNY whispers a figure into KATO's ear. KATO whispers into CHESTER's ear. CHESTER whispers into DEEDEE's ear.)*

DeeDee: What?!

Chester and **Kato** (covering her mouth): Shh!

Chester *(to BENNY)*: We have to talk it over. *(They huddle.)*

Kato: We can't afford that! All I've got on me is 37 cents.

Chester: I only have $2.53 at home, and I was saving it for a rainy day.

DeeDee: Don't look at me! I don't have any money.

Chester: We only need it for one day! *(He gets a bright idea and turns to BENNY.)* We thought it over, and we would like it, but we'd have to take it for a test drive first.

Benny: Well . . .

DeeDee: I thought we only needed it for one . . . *(KATO stops her before she spills the beans.)*

Benny: What . . . ?

Kato: Umm. . . . We only need one test drive and then we'll decide!

Chester: We'll be back soon.

Kato: Just once around the millennium, you know.

Benny: All right. Don't be long! *(He exits.)*

★ *The kids go over to the machine.*

DeeDee: Wow! A real time machine.

Kato: What do we do now?

DeeDee: Simple! Don't you see? If we can go back in time and convince people to stop littering and cutting down trees, then their children won't . . . and their children won't . . . and their children won't . . . and their children won't either.

Chester: That's a great idea, DeeDee!

DeeDee: It is?

Kato: Sure! But we don't have much time. We'll have to visit very famous people—so the whole world can learn from their example.

DeeDee: Where should we go first?

Chester: Let's do something to clean up the harbors, rivers, oceans, and ponds!

Kato: Let's see. Who were the first people to pollute the water?

Chester: I've got it!

★ *The three of them pop into the time machine and it takes off.*

★ *GRANDPA GARBAGE emerges from the corner where he has been hiding all along.*

Grandpa Garbage: So, they think that they can clean up the past, do they? They want to get rid of all my beautiful garbage, do they? They think they're the only ones who can get a time machine, do they? Well, do they?

★ *BENNY enters.*

Benny: Did someone say that they needed a time machine?

Grandpa Garbage: What?

Benny: Benny's the name. I sell time machines— new and used. I also got watches. *(BENNY rolls up his jacket sleeve to show his watches.)*

Grandpa Garbage: I need a time machine!

Benny: You're in luck. I got my last one—still available. Step this way. I'll show it to ya!

★ *They exit.*

★ *End of Scene*

Scene 3

The Boston Tea Party

★ *Time: Year 1773*

★ *The stage is set to look like a dock as if the water is beyond the downstage edge where the audience is sitting. A rope can be set up across the front of the stage about three feet high to show the edge of the dock. Fishing nets and coiled rope can be used to decorate the upstage areas. There are three large crates downstage right that have the word "TEA" painted on the side. The colonists JEAN, TOM, and MARNIE enter, in traditional Native American dress.*

Jean: This new land promises great freedoms for all colonists.

Tom: I see great happiness here. We shall overcome the oppression of the King!

★ *PETE runs on. He is dressed in traditional Native American dress. He has a headband without a feather.*

Pete: We are almost ready for you. Do you have the feathers?

Jean: Yes, here they are. *(She hands him some feathers.)*

Tom: Is all of the tea loaded on the boat?

Pete: Oh, yes! The boat is full of tea!

★ SAM *and* JESSICA *enter.*

Sam: Pete, we are ready!

Jessica: Those Redcoats will be surprised when we toss their tea in the harbor!

Pete: We will show them that our freedom will not be threatened by taxes on tea.

Sam: We will gladly go without tea for a year rather than pay their tax!

Jessica: We will go without tea for ten years!

Marnie: I will gladly give up tea for fifteen years.

Jean: I like tea. I have six cups a day—very hot with cream and sugar. I especially like it in the morning with a biscuit and orange marmalade.

Jessica: Don't you want to put an end to the oppression of the King?

Pete: We have to make a statement!

Jean: Couldn't we just send him a letter?

Marnie *(pointing offstage)*: Look!

Tom: Where?

Jean: Look at that house that has fallen from the sky . . . next to the ship.

Tom: Is it a demon?

Marnie: Or a spirit?

★ *CHESTER, DEEDEE, and KATO enter.*

Chester: Hello!

DeeDee and **Kato:** Hi!

Pete: Who are you?

Chester: My name is Chester.

Sam: Are you a demon?

Jessica: Or a spirit?

Chester: I'm just a kid.

Jean: What about your friends? Are they spirits?

Kato: No! We've come to convince you not to spill the tea into the harbor.

Marnie: They must be redcoats!

Tom: But how would the redcoats know that we were going to spill the tea?

Jean: Spies!

DeeDee: No! We are Americans!

Pete: You don't look like anyone I know.

Kato: That's not important. We don't have much time.

Chester: You can't put all that tea in the water. You'll pollute it!

Jessica: But we have to make a statement.

Pete: We are being taxed unfairly.

Kato: Boycott the tax. Refuse to pay it! If you dump all that tea into the water, where will it go? Who will clean it up? Think of the fish.

DeeDee: The fish might not even be thirsty!

Kato: What if everyone just went around dumping things into the water?

Chester: Think how dirty it would become.

Tom: I like to swim in the water. I wouldn't like to swim in a place full of garbage.

Marnie: I wash my clothes with the same water. I would not like to wash clothes with dirty water.

Jean: And I like tea! Why waste it? If you are spirits we thank you for your guidance.

Chester: We're glad to help. Come on.

★ *He exits with the other kids.*

Jean: Well, now what should we do?

Tom: Let's go over to my house. Maybe we'll see

Paul Revere.

Jean: Did you hear his latest? Last night he opened his window and yelled, "The British are humming! The British are humming!"

Tom: Humming? What were they humming?

Jean: "God Save the King" no doubt!

★ *They all laugh and exit.*

★ *GRANDPA GARBAGE sneaks on and dumps the tea into the harbor, himself.*

Grandpa Garbage: Little cleanies!

★ *End of Scene*

Scene 4

George Washington's Hill

★ *Time: Year 1738*

★ GEORGE *and his* MOM *enter.*

Mom: Now, George, you pick all the ripe cherries from the tree.

George: All of them?

Mom: Oh yes. I promised some to Aunt Louise and Uncle Sebastian. I should also send some over to Noonie and Ah-hah.

George: Noonie and Ah-hah? They have their own cherry tree! And Noonie always pinches my cheeks and always calls me Georgie-Porgie. Why can't they eat their own cherries?

Mom: Well, they're getting old, dear. They don't have a big strong son to reach the high ones. Oh, I almost forgot the Jeffersons. Better pick another peck for them. Proceed to pick your pecks, George.

★ *She exits.*

George *(Imitating his mother in a voice too soft for her to hear)*: Proceed to pick your pecks, George.

★ CHESTER, DEEDEE, *and* KATO *enter.*

Chester *(pointing at* GEORGE*)*: There he is! Let's wait back here and see what happens.

DeeDee: That's the father of our country? He looks a little young.

Chester: This is when he was still a boy. He cut down a cherry tree.

DeeDee: Why?

Kato: I don't know—but we'd better find out if we want to stop him.

George *(talking to himself)*: Every year it's the same thing. Pick the cherries, pick the cherries, all day, every day. I wish I didn't have this stupid tree. *(George swings his ax and is about to chop down the tree.)*

DeeDee *(crossing down to GEORGE)*: That's not very nice. Trees are important.

George: Who are you?

DeeDee: I am a friend of all trees.

George: Well, this tree is not my friend. Every year it grows cherries, and every year I have to pick them. I'd much rather be playing. I don't even like cherries.

DeeDee: This tree is helping you breathe.

George: It is? How?

DeeDee: Trees give us oxygen.

George: Who cares about oxygen?

★ *KATO comes down to meet them.*

Kato: Who cares about oxygen?

George: Who are you?

Kato: A friend of oxygen.

George: Who needs oxygen?

37

Kato: We all need oxygen to live!

DeeDee: Animals need oxygen too! Dogs, cats, cows, goats, horses . . .

George: Even duckies?

★ *DEEDEE, CHESTER, and KATO look at each other.*

DeeDee: Especially duckies!

Chester: The air is getting more and more polluted. We need trees to clean up the air!

George *(still thinking about the duckies)*: Even duckies need oxygen? I wouldn't like to cut down the tree if it would mean less oxygen for duckies. I will not cut it down. I will pick the pecks that mother asked for. With each peck I shall think of the little duckies that are breathing the oxygen from my tree.

Kato: That's great. We have to go now. We're running out of time!

DeeDee: It was nice meeting you, Mr. President.

George: Oh no, my last name is Washington.

DeeDee: Oh, sorry. 'Bye.

★ *They exit.*

George: I'd better go around back and get the cherry baskets.

★ *He exits. GRANDPA GARBAGE enters and chops down the cherry tree. He cackles in delight and exits.*

★ *End of Scene*

Scene 5

Dodo Island

★ *Time: 1500s*

★ *There are three trees placed across center stage—one left, one right, and one exactly center. The center tree is the one that the Dodos will circle later in the scene. The tree should be colorful and taller than the tallest actor in the play. The temperature on the island is very hot. Actors should imagine that the ground is covered with sand.*

★ *CHESTER, KATO, DEEDEE enter the stage from the time machine.*

DeeDee: Where are we?

Kato: I don't know. I just punched in "extinct animals" and this is where we ended up.

Chester: I wonder what year we're in.

DeeDee: Someone's coming.

Chester: Let's wait back here out of sight.

★ *The three of them hide near the back of the stage.*

★ *DOTTY, a Dodo bird, comes out.*

Dotty: Food. *Wok!* Food. *Wok! Wok! (She continues to search for food. She occasionally bumps into objects.)*

Chester: Could it be? I think it is . . .

Kato: Is what? Is what?

Chester: That, my friends, is an Apoxicus Dobirdacus.

DeeDee: Acopa what? Daberda who?

Chester: A Dodo bird.

DeeDee: Let's go talk to it.

Chester: No, we might scare it. Let's watch a little longer.

★ *DIZZY enters looking worried.*

Dizzy: Did you find him?

41

Dotty: No. *Wok!* I've been looking behind this tree for hours.

Dizzy: You looked for him behind this tree?

Dotty: I cannot get behind it.

Dizzy: And why not?

Dotty: I have spent a long time looking behind this tree for him. Yet, every time I go behind the tree, I look and there is suddenly another side to go behind. Just watch. Let's look for him behind this tree. *(They both walk around the tree.)* Now look! There is still another side to go behind.

Dizzy: Then let us go behind it. *(They walk back to the downstage side of the tree.)* I see your dilemma.

★ *DINGY enters.*

Dingy: There you both are. Have you found him?

Dotty: No. We are trying to look behind this tree, yet it is quite impossible.

Dizzy: What if he is behind the tree and we never know?

Dingy: Oh, our poor baby brother.

★ *DAFFY enters. DIZZY crosses to him.*

Dizzy: Have you found our baby brother yet?

Daffy: We're still searching for him. Have you?

Dizzy: Mama will not be happy if we can't find Baby.

Daffy: She will scold us for sure.

Dizzy: We must not dawdle. We must discover some way to get behind this tree.

★ *CHESTER, DEEDEE and KATO are watching this scene.*

Chester *(to DEEDEE)*: The Dodo birds are extinct now.

DeeDee *(to CHESTER)*: What does extinct mean?

Chester: It means that they aren't anymore. There are none left.

DeeDee: Where are they?

Kato: They didn't survive.

DeeDee: Is that what people mean when they talk about endangered species?

Chester: Those are animals that are in danger of not surviving. They can't adapt to the changing environment.

DeeDee: They're not smart enough to adapt?

Kato: In some places in 1993, DeeDee, man is destroying the environment so fast that the animals have no place to live or get food.

DeeDee: That's terrible. How can we help?

Chester: Well, maybe if we take a Dodo bird back with us to 1993, it can tell us what's different about the way we live in the future.

DeeDee: Let's do it. We'd be the only kids with a pet Dodo!

Kato: Which Dodo should we bring back with us?

Chester: Maybe we should look for this baby Dodo. Then we could teach it all about the future—and it could lead a happy, long life!

Kato: Well, let's look around!

★ *The three of them exit.*

★ *MAMA DODO BIRD comes on searching.*

Mama: My poor baby. I miss him so. A child so young needs his mother to help and keep him, to teach him the way. Like my dear mother taught me and her dear mother taught her and her mother taught her and her mother taught her and her mother . . . . *(to audience)* Can you see the pattern here? You see . . .

A Dodo's a bird like no other;
It should not be apart from its mother.
It will sniffle so sadly
And feel, well, quite badly.
And its wings do not fly, soar, or hover.

My poor baby! *(Runs off crying.)*

★ *BABY wanders in.*

Baby: If I walk 72 steps this way and 49 steps that way, I am sure to be back at the nest.

★ *CHESTER, DEEDEE, and KATO walk in.*

Chester: Look—there it is! The baby Dodo bird!

DeeDee: Grab him!

Kato: No, DeeDee. We have to talk to him. Tell him about our plan.

DeeDee: Then grab him?

Chester: No, DeeDee! We have to convince him that it is a good idea for him to come with us to 1993.

DeeDee: How are we going to do that? We only have a few more minutes left before we have to return the time machine to Benny!

Kato: What are we wasting time for? Let's go talk to the bird! *(She crosses to BABY.)* Hi, I'm Kato.

Baby: I'm lost. I'm looking for the rest of my family. Are you lost too?

Chester: No. Why do you ask?

Baby: I've never seen you around here before.

Kato: We're not from around here. We're from the

future.

Baby: Is that farther than the farthest mountain?

DeeDee: Oh, yes. We're from another time!

Chester: We've come to bring you back with us.

Kato: We are from the year 1993.

Baby: That is far away. What happens in 1993? Are there many successful Dodos there?

Chester: Not exactly.

DeeDee: Actually, the Dodo has become extinct at the time we are from. There are no more of you.

Chester: That is why we want you to come back with us and give the Dodo a future.

Baby: Would I be very popular?

Chester: Oh, yes! When people hear that there is a real Dodo in 1993, they will certainly stop and take notice.

Baby: Then I will go with you. I have many

sisters, and I often get lost in the shuffle. That is how I became lost today.

Chester: Come on, guys. Let's bring the baby Dodo back to 1993 with us and see what effects our Boston Tea Party and George Washington work has had.

★ *They exit with* BABY.

★ *End of Scene*

Scene 6

The Pond

★ *Time: Year 1993*

★ *The pond is still in the same mess that the kids left it in. The work that they did in the time machine did nothing to help the environment.*

Kato *(running on)*: Here we are, back at the great, big, beautiful . . . *(looking around)* polluted, dirty, garbage pond!

Chester: I don't understand it. I thought that we could make a difference! All of our hard work and traveling was for nothing!

DeeDee: I don't get it. Why didn't it help? I thought that we were coming back to a brand new and improved 1993. Instead, it is just as dirty and polluted as we left it.

Chester: So much for time travel chain reactions.

Kato: I can't believe that we did all that for nothing.

★ *They all sit in despair amidst the pollution.*

DeeDee: Well, at least we have a pet Dodo bird!

Baby *(sneezing)*: *A-choo! A-choo!* I can't stop . . . *A-choo!* sneezing! *A-choo!*

Kato: What's the matter with him?

Baby: *A-choo!* This isn't as fun as I thought, *A-choo!*, it would be! *A-choo!*

Chester: Maybe he's allergic to the air. After all, nothing we did in the time machine did anything to make the land, water, or air any cleaner!

Baby: *A-choo!* I want my, *A-choo!*, mommy! *(BABY starts to cry and sneeze at the same time.)*

DeeDee: What are we going to do now? Baby wants his mommy!

Chester: We better send him back home. I can set the controls on the time machine to bring Baby back to his nest and then return itself to Benny. *(to BABY)* Come on, Baby. You're going home.

★ CHESTER *and* BABY *exit.*

★ GRANDMA *and* GRANDCHILD *enter in their own time machine.)*

Grandchild: Look, Grandma. There they are!

Kato: Who are you?

Grandma: We're from the future. We came to help.

Chester *(entering)*: Well, Baby's on his way back home. *(to* GRANDMA *and* GRANDCHILD*)* Who are you?

Grandchild: We know about all of your travels.

Grandma: We just wanted to tell you that you are wasting your time.

Chester: We know!

DeeDee: We tried to go back and change things but it didn't work.

Kato: I guess that some things never change.

Grandma: Well, some things DO!

DeeDee: What do you mean?

51

Grandma: You are concentrating on changing the wrong thing. You have to do something in your own time.

Grandchild: Don't try to change things in somebody else's time!

Grandma: The future is yours. You must make of it what you will. Act today to clean the world for tomorrow.

Chester: I get it! We can only make changes today for tomorrow!

Kato: Don't change yesterday for today!

Chester: What is past is past! We can't fix it.

Kato: We are in charge of what happens today!

DeeDee: I don't get it!

Grandchild: We have to pick up trash and recycle and save trees and animals today so we can enjoy them tomorrow and the day after and the day after and all the days after that.

DeeDee: Wow! You're so smart! It sometimes takes me a while to catch on to things. I guess that will never change.

Chester: Hey, everybody, let's clean up!

★ *GRANDPA GARBAGE enters.*

Grandpa Garbage: No! Don't clean up! Don't clean up my beautiful garbage! If you clean up the earth, you'll destroy me!

★ *No one listens to him and they continue to clean.*

Kato: Hey, this place is looking better already.

Chester: There's just one big piece of garbage to get rid of.

★ *DEEDEE wheels on a big garbage can with a phony lid made of paper so the actor can later break through it.*

DeeDee: Ready!

★ *CHESTER, DEEDEE, and KATO help GRANDPA GARBAGE into the trash can.*

Grandpa Garbage: No! Not my beautiful garbage! Not the can! Anything but the can!

★ *The kids put on the lid.*

Chester, DeeDee, Kato: Done!

★ *At that moment the actor playing* GRANDPA
   GARBAGE *breaks through the top of the trash
   can. He has taken off his outer coat of garbage
   and is dressed like a regular kid.*

Kato: Who are you?

Grandpa Garbage: Well, I used to be Grandpa
Garbage, but, before that, I was just a kid. I
remember my mom telling me that if I didn't
clean up after myself and stop littering I'd become
a "Grandpa Garbage." I didn't know what she
meant. I thought everybody littered. Then, one
day I woke up and there was garbage all over my
room. I did become a Grandpa Garbage! I don't
know how it happened, maybe it has something to
do with the time travel, but I'm young again! I've
got another chance, and I'll never pollute again!

★ *They all cheer!*

★ GRANDMA *and* GRANDCHILD *come downstage
   away from the group.*

Grandchild: Where are *you*, Grandma?

Grandma: What do you mean?

Grandchild: You said that you knew these kids in 1993. Here we are in 1993. Where are you? We want to see what you looked like when you were a kid. *(realizing)* Your first name is Deirdre, isn't it?

Grandma: Oh, yes. But when I was young, they used to call me DeeDee.

Grandchild: Wow! Things can change, Grandma! Things can change!

★ *Curtain*

Douglas Love began his career in theater as a child actor and grew up in show business, appearing in more than fifty productions. He has produced five national tours in more than seventy cities across the United States. Mr. Love is the author of *Blame It on the Wolf*, *Holiday in the Rain Forest*, and *Kabuki Gift*, all published by HarperCollins. He is also the coauthor of the stage adaptation of *Free to Be . . . You and Me*. Mr. Love is on the faculty of The Children's Theater School in Milwaukee, Wisconsin, and is a guest teacher at the school's Summer Theater Workshop in Vail, Colorado. Mr. Love lives in New York City.

God gives conviction—and ***always accompanies it with a solution.***

Conviction in our hearts brings repentance.

God not only convicts us, He leads us to confession and repentance.

If there is someone we need to love, forgive or apologize to, He tells us.

If there is something we are neglecting that we need to make a priority in our lives, He tells us.

If the world has crept in and is robbing us of a closer walk with Him, He tells us.

If we need to come apart and rest awhile, He tells us.

If sin is hindering our close fellowship with Him, He instructs us to confess it and forsake it.

But condemnation...it is guilt without a solution. It comes from the enemy of our souls to wear us down when we are already worn out. Discouragement settles into our spirits.

Our pace slows to a crawl....

Chapter 5

God's Servant

Constant criticism wears us down and steals our joy. It seems our congregations will not and cannot ever be satisfied with anything we do. There is always a long list of things we have left undone. We know it and they know it.

Though they have never pastored; preached a sermon; conducted a funeral; dealt with the tensions of a wedding; put a church back together after a vicious split; stood against the constant bombardment of the devil who is determined to "smite the shepherd so the sheep will be scattered;" agonized over a decision that is going to be costly and will involve souls; been on call 365 days a year, 24 hours a day; and never faced the unceasing criticisms from the congregation—they have *all* the answers, in *every* situation of exactly what we should do; what we should wear; where we should live; what car we should drive; what music we should sing; what prayers we should pray; what sermons we should preach; what we should do with our leisure time; how many hours (if any) we should sleep; where we should go on vacation (it makes little difference, as we are too tired to enjoy it); how much we should weigh; how our children should behave; and whose hand we should shake first.

And woe be unto us if we ever reprove and rebuke when things get nasty.

The average church member wants

a leader who does not lead;

a pastor who is never discouraged;

a human who has no need of rest or sleep.

Can we be what the people want us to be? **Never.**

Can we be what **we** want us to be? **Never.**

Can we be what the Lord wants us to be? Unbelievably— yes!

We can simply listen to His voice—

not the complaining voices of men—

not the accusing voice of Satan—

not even our own accusing voice—

but day by day,

moment by moment,

do what God

tells us to do.

Jesus said, "My sheep hear my voice, and I know them, and **_they follow me_**."

We must realize we cannot do everything by ourselves. We will never please our critics. Yes, a shepherd is yoked to his flock, and daily responsibilities come with that yoke.

However, a pastor will never fulfill the people's expectations of him.

A pastor's wife will be unable to fulfill the expectations of the people. What satisfies some of the members will infuriate others.

A pastor's children will never be able to be the model children that the congregation wants them to be. Parents are instructed to train their children, because they arrive needing training. **All children arrive this way.** Unfortunately, this includes pastor's children.

It is impossible to please the people. God instructs His people not to be "...menpleasers; but as the servants of Christ, doing **the will of God** from the heart; with good will doing service, **as to the Lord, and not to men.**" *Ephesians 6:6-7*

Our one priority is to listen to the still small voice of our Shepherd and follow Him. **His** yoke is the **only** yoke that is easy.

If you have pleased Him, it is enough.

He is our Master. We are His servants. When we become His servants, we become servants and ministers, not **of** mankind, but **to** mankind.

The question is asked of the congregation in Romans 14:4: "Who art thou that judgest another man's servant? To his own master he standeth or falleth...."

Many Members—One Body

"So we, being **many, are one** body in Christ."

Jesus did not attempt to please the people. In fact, He displeased them so much that they crucified Him.

Peter wrote, "...ye should follow his steps." *I Peter 2:21*

How did our Lord walk?

He tells us: "...I do always **_those things that please him._**"

This is the only way we will survive the ministry.

God's Word commands us to do a multitude of things, including going into all the world and preaching the gospel to every creature. God has shown us the only way to accomplish our tasks. He calls on the body of Christ to do His work.

"...ye are the body of Christ, and members in particular."

God expects His work to get done on this earth. He expects the sick, the imprisoned, the hungry, the sinners, the heartbroken, the feeble-minded, the widows, the aged, and the backslidden to be ministered to. But He expects His entire body to do the work, not one man, who has been hired by lazy and complacent people, to do it all. Yes, every church has a group of faithful, willing workers. But the harvest is great and the laborers too few, in the church as a whole and in each church in particular.

God's Word compares His body to our bodies.

Our eyes do not do everything. They are required only to see.

Our ears do not do everything. They were created only to hear.

Our toes do not do everything. They were made to help us keep our balance while walking.

Even our mouth does not do everything!

If a pastor has been hired by a congregation made up of shiftless members, he will soon fall far short of their expectations. They know there is work to do, but they expect the pastor to do everything in their church, neighborhood, and city. They have hired him to do their praying, studying, teaching, witnessing and visiting.

Do you remember what drove our Lord to fashion a whip and drive people from the temple? The people who were supposed to bring a sacrifice were **buying** a sacrifice! What angered Jesus then is sure to anger Him today. People buy a pastor to be their sacrifice, while they remain idle and the fields remain unharvested. It is not God's plan!

The pastor will wear himself out as he attempts to prepare the field, purchase the seed, sow the seed, pray for the rain, pray for the sunshine, pray away the storms, harvest the crops, prepare the food for consumption and then distribute the food to the hungry.

Many people, again in our day, want to go to the temple and give money to purchase their sacrifice. They offer their purchased pastor to the Lord. They do nothing themselves in the field of harvest. It is not God's way! It will doom their pastor to failure. The pastor will wear out. All the work cannot possibly get done. One man cannot do it. A few men cannot do it. It takes the entire body, each functioning as God ordains, to fulfill the work of God in a church and in a city.

When all the needs are not met and jobs remain undone, complainers will begin to complain and critics will begin to criticize. Soon there is an undercurrent of tension in the church. Telephones begin to ring.

"Don't you think our church would do better with a new pastor? This one seems pretty worn out."

Countless pastors have been fired by their parishioners at least once. The chance of a pastor being fired is now higher than the chance of a football coach being fired.

The disheartened pastor will begin anew with more unreasonable demands and more impossible expectations—

in another church;

with another congregation.

Chapter 6

Down in the Valley

Unfulfilled hopes begin to weigh on a pastor until he sags under a heavy burden of discouragement. Many pastors descend into the valley of despair. The descent into the valley is not a sudden thud. One day he wakes up and finds he is no longer living on the mountain. Somehow he has fallen to the depths of the valley and has no strength to begin the climb out.

The valleys come to everyone's life.

Loved ones die.
Friendships fail.
Hopes fade.
God's promises tarry.

While others mourn, the pastor comforts. When a church disturbance comes, the pastor tries to ignore the hurt in his own heart while mending his wounded sheep.

The view in the valley isn't very good. We are surrounded by mountains that we are too weary to climb. The sun isn't shining as brightly. Then comes the nagging question that robs us of joy and sleep:

"What are we doing down here anyway? We're supposed to be happy!"

Condemnation creeps into our thoughts.

How can we effectively pastor while sitting in a valley—discouraged—staring at mountains all around us and dreading the climb out?

What is wrong with us?

Who are we to pastor others?

If anyone still wonders if pastors face temptation, the answer is YES! The biggest temptation of every pastor is to give up and quit!

Did you know that Martin Luther was tempted to quit in despair? He taught the Scriptures to his congregation at a rapid pace, determined to pack them full of the Word of God. This was his weekly teaching schedule:

Sunday at 5:00 a.m.	**Pauline Epistles**
Sunday at 9:00 a.m.	**The Gospels**
Sunday Afternoon	**The Catechism**
Monday	**The Catechism**
Tuesday	**The Catechism**
Wednesday	**The Gospel of Matthew**
Thursday	**The Epistles**
Friday	**The Epistles**
Saturday	**The Gospel of John**

(Hunger for God's Word is sadly lacking in today's church. Who would gather to hear Luther's teachings in our day? Three services a week are an overload for most congregations.)

Luther not only taught the Bible and preached his sermons, he sang, strummed his lute and played his flute. He penned over 60,000 pages of Bible teachings. He turned his entire congregation into his choir. He married Katherina, a feisty, redheaded, twenty-six year old ex-nun when he was forty-two. (He made the comment to a friend, "If I should ever marry again, I would hew myself an obedient wife out of stone.")

Martin and Katie had six noisy children. They adopted four more noisy children. Martin brought home needy students, the homeless, the sick and the dying. Katie took care of the orchard, fish pond, barnyard, harvested the fruit, caught the fish and slaughtered the pigs. She fed twenty-five or thirty people around her table daily. Martin gave away what money he had and never concerned himself with the problem of feeding his household. He left that to God and Katie.

We read about Martin and Katie's lives and feel worthless. How did they keep such a pace? Did Martin ever get discouraged?

He did. He retreated to his valley (in his case, his study) more than once, bowed down with depression. He would refuse to come out, locking himself in for three days at a time. Katie would put up with it for a while, but when she'd had enough of his gloom, she simply removed the door from the hinges.

Once when Katie noticed a deep discouragement settling over her husband, she tried as she usually did to cheer him, but nothing she did worked. Martin was unwilling to begin his climb out of the valley.

He was bombarded with betrayals and misunderstandings of friends. Vicious rumors surrounded him. He was branded a heathen, called a wild boar and denounced as the devil incarnate. Martin grew tired of the unreasonable hatred of his enemies and constant death threats. Adding to his misery was his poor health.

His eyes lost their glow and his pace slowed to a crawl. A deep depression settled within him. Friends tried to encourage him, but he was too weary to listen to their counsel.

Katie decided it was time to act. He heard her wails the moment he entered the house. He discovered her dressed in mourning clothes, too lost in grief to even notice him.

"Who died, Katie?" he cried. "Who died?"

She finally quit sobbing enough to gasp, "Oh, Martin! God is dead! I can't bear it, for all His work is overthrown!"

Martin's face flushed in anger. "That is utter blasphemy, Katherina!" he raged.

Her sobs stopped and her voice grew stern. "Martin, you have been going around acting as if God is dead, as if God is no longer here to keep us. So I thought I ought to put on mourning to keep you company in your great bereavement."

Martin Luther got back to work.

Luther was 47 years old when he became totally disgusted with his complacent congregation. He decided to go on strike. Instead of his usual Sunday sermon, Luther announced, "I refuse to preach to you. You remain godless. It annoys me to keep preaching to you. When you mend

50

your ways, I will return to my pulpit."

They mended.

He returned.

Charles H. Spurgeon said of Martin Luther: "...he was by no means of the weaker sort. His great spirit was often in seventh heaven of exultation, and as frequently on the borders of despair."

Charles Spurgeon said of himself while praying, "Lord, end my winter, and let my spring begin. I cannot with all my longing raise my soul out of her death and dullness, but all things are possible with Thee."

Spurgeon spoke of the critics who take out their penknives to gore and gash and added, "As it is recorded that David, in the heat of battle, waxed faint, so it may be written of all of the servants of the Lord. Fits of depression come over the most of us."

He also stated, "For my part, I am quite willing to be eaten by dogs for the next fifty years; but the more distant future shall vindicate me."

Today Spurgeon is referred to as "The Prince of Preachers." During his lifetime, he was often castigated— even despised—for his unyielding stance on crucial matters of Biblical principle. John F. MacArthur, Jr. said of Spurgeon: "His willingness to stand firm in the face of such hostility is the key to Spurgeon's real greatness."

It should encourage every pastor to know that he is not alone. David Wilkerson wrote about the ministers' gatherings he holds throughout Africa, South America, and Central America. Pastors there work a secular job to support themselves while pastoring. He says they are discouraged and wounded.

Chapter 7

The Beloved Wolf

Many pastors in America are not only discouraged and wounded; they are quitting. We all have heard at least one pastor say: "I quit! I don't have to put up with this! I'm going to sell cars...shoes...refrigerators...insurance... anything but this!"

If you have been called by God to work in His field, don't quit. When God calls a messenger, it is a calling without repentance. God expects His messengers to run the race straight into heaven—our one and only finish line.

A man called to service by God will trust God to supply his needs. He will follow the example left by Jesus. He will lay down his life daily for the sheep God has entrusted to His care.

Only hirelings quit. A hireling works only for a paycheck.

Jesus said, "he that is an hireling, and not the shepherd, whose own the sheep are not, **seeth the wolf coming**, and leaveth the sheep, and fleeth: and the wolf catcheth them, and scattereth the sheep. The hireling fleeth, because he is an hireling, and careth not for the sheep." *John 10:12-13*

When the wolf enters a church, he comes for one purpose—to eat sheep. Every sheep and every lamb is vulnerable to his attack.

Paul warned us about these times. "For I know this, that after my departing shall grievous wolves enter in among you, not sparing the flock."

Wolves.

They dress up in sheep's clothing. They work like sheep do, sing in the choir with the sheep, outwardly look like sheep, smell like sheep, bleat like sheep and act like sheep. And the sheep befriend the wolves who look just like them.

But one day, the shepherd sees the teeth of a wolf under the mask. Because of his love for the defenseless sheep, he attacks the wolf.

The bleating of the sheep join in a loud cry:

"Our pastor has attacked a sheep! What is wrong with our pastor?"

The pastor says, "This is a bad wolf that has come to eat you."

The congregation says, "This is a sheep. You are the wolf!"

The shepherd stays and endures the onslaught against him. But the hireling gives up, runs from the church and his ungrateful sheep. He may have battled wolves for years, but suddenly he has had it. The sheep, deceived by the costume that disguises the wolf, inevitably pity the wolf. Thus, the sheep become easy prey. The wolf devours them, one by one.

If the shepherd stays in the church to protect his sheep, the wolf leaves. But invariably, some of the sheep will follow the wolf out the door.

The only reason a pastor will remain with his flock during these times is because he truly cares for God's sheep.

"The hireling fleeth, because he is an hireling, and **careth not for the sheep**."

A pastor, called of God, will stay and endure the criticism from the flock for dealing with the wolf. He stays because there are precious, beloved sheep under his care that he loves so much he will sacrifice his own life for them.

Smite the Shepherd

Enemies of the church know how to destroy a flock. The formula they use is revealed to us in the Bible:

"Smite the shepherd, and the sheep shall be scattered." *Zechariah 13:7; Matthew 26:31; Mark 14:27*

Smite the shepherd....

Smite means to **beat, smack, torment, hit, strike, afflict, plague, grieve, or distress**.

Every shepherd will be smitten—lied about, talked about, criticized, hated, and ridiculed. Some shepherds will not endure these grievous times. When they leave their flocks, the sheep will be scattered. Many sheep will not be found in any church within six months.

The constant attack is unleashed against the shepherd.

If *a sheep* is attacked, *a sheep* will be destroyed.

If *a shepherd* is destroyed, *a flock* will be destroyed.

If *a pastor* is destroyed, *a church* will be destroyed.

Pastors do not enjoy being smitten. However, every pastor who is called by God to care for God's flock will be smitten—over and over and over again.

Jesus warns us that we "...resist not evil: but whosoever shall **smite thee** on thy right cheek, turn to him the other also." *Matthew 5:39*

The temptation is to smite back.

The temptation is to quit being a target for the smiters.

The temptation is to quit pastoring.

Turning the cheek means to make ourselves vulnerable to be smitten again. In other words, we stay in the ministry, knowing we will have to continuously endure being slapped.

Our Lord, the Good Shepherd, left us an Example.

"For even hereunto were ye called: because Christ also suffered for us, leaving us an example, that **ye should follow his steps**: Who did no sin, neither was guile found in his mouth: Who, when he was reviled, reviled not again; when he suffered, he threatened not; but committed himself to him that judgeth righteously." *I Peter 2:21-23*

The wolves gathered together to mock and ridicule Jesus even as His blood poured from His tortured body. He could have left the cross. If He had, the entire human race would be doomed.   He chose instead to remain on the cross and endure the scorn and the shame.

Have you entered the ministry to proclaim the name of Jesus Christ?   Do you intend to invite your listeners to the foot of the cross to have their sins washed away? The scorners are still gathered there, mocking, ridiculing, despising, jeering.   Today they despise the servants of Jesus.

"Proud and haughty scorner is his name, who dealeth in proud wrath." *Proverbs 21:24*

You can walk away. But your choice may result in many souls going into eternity unsaved.

The great Apostle Paul told us about his life of endurance.

"I am...in labours more abundant, in stripes above measure, in prisons more frequent, in deaths oft...five times received I forty stripes save one. Thrice was I beaten with rods, once was I stoned, thrice I suffered shipwreck, a night and a day I have been in the deep; in journeyings often, in perils of waters, in perils of robbers, in perils by mine own countrymen, in perils by the heathen, in perils in the city, in perils in the wilderness, in perils in the sea, in perils among false brethren; in weariness and painfulness, in watchings often, in hunger and thirst, in fastings often, in cold and nakedness.   Beside those things that are without, **that which cometh upon me daily, the care of all the churches.**" *II Corinthians 11:23-28*

Paul summed up his commitment just before he was killed: "***I have fought*** ... ***I have finished***...***I have kept***."

Seeking a Following

After we receive the warning about the wolves entering in among the church, Paul adds: "*Also of your own selves shall men arise, speaking perverse things, to draw away disciples after them.*" *Acts 20:30*

Every pastor has seen it time and again. Someone rises up out of the congregation, seeking a following. It matters not how long the pastor has loved the sheep and cared for them.

One who seeks glory for himself rises up out of the congregation, desiring sheep to follow him, rather than the shepherd. Invariably, some of the sheep will turn on their pastor and follow another out the door of the church.

The sheep seldom even listen to the message spoken by the one they are following. (The message usually consists of one theme: "The pastor is bad.") The sheep don't care that they are following one who is "speaking perverse things." The sheep don't realize that the one they are following cares nothing about protecting them from harm. The sheep do not discern the glory-seeker's self-centered motives.

"Of your own selves shall men arise...*to draw away disciples after them....*"

The glory-seeker seeks disciples for himself, not for Jesus. As the pastor views the exodus, he feels rejected by the sheep he has cared for and loved. He grieves for the sheep. He prays the sheep that have left will find a shepherd who will love them enough to watch over their souls.

Chapter 8

Seeking a Miracle

"And a great multitude followed him, **because they saw his miracles** which he did on them that were diseased." *John 6:2*

Just as people followed Jesus for different reasons, people come to church for various reasons. Some come during their time of need. When they no longer need the pastor's prayers for a miracle, the pastor's counsel, the church's financial help, the use of the sanctuary for a wedding or a funeral, letters sent to a prisoner, or visits to a hospital bed, they leave the church. The excuse for leaving is never, "I only came because I needed something from the church. I left when I got it!"

Their excuse will more likely be that the pastor is rude, unfriendly, did or said something they didn't agree with, or didn't do or say something they thought he should have done or said. The mean pastor is blamed for their self-centeredness.

Seeking a Meal

Jesus looked over the multitude who followed Him and said: "Ye seek me, not because ye saw the miracles, but because ye did eat of the loaves, and were filled. Labour not for the meat which perisheth, but for that meat which endureth unto everlasting life...He that eateth my flesh, and drinketh my blood, dwelleth in me, and I in him. This is that bread which came down from heaven: not as your fathers did eat manna, and are dead: he that eateth of this bread shall live forever. From that time **many of his disciples went back, and walked no more with him.**" *John 6:26-27, 56, 58, 66*

This crowd did not seek a Savior who could give them eternal life. They came only for a meal. Food and fellowship were sufficient. They had no desire to hear what He could give them after they died. What did He have for them **now?** When their stomachs were full and the conversation changed to spiritual things, they left.

The crowds today are no different. Among them are the ones who drift into the church for food and fellowship. When the talk gets too spiritual, they leave. Why stay? Their stomachs are full. **"Ye did eat of the loaves, and were filled...."**

Jesus said of the crowd who came for their miracle or their meal: "...many believed in his name, when they saw the miracles which he did. But Jesus did not commit himself unto them, because he knew all men." *John 2:23-24*

John knew why they were part of His crowd. He did not commit *(obligate)* Himself unto them because He knew that they did not commit themselves unto Him. The following verse says, *"...he knew what was in man."*

Unfortunately, pastors often do commit themselves unto these people. They commit their friendship, their love, their trust, and their time. When one walks away from what the pastor believed was a mutual friendship, the pastor feels rejected. Each time this happens, he finds it a little harder to commit himself to someone else.

Seeking a Rest

Some come into the church and dedicate themselves wholeheartedly to the work. Pastors are thrilled that someone has come to labor rather than to rest; to give, rather than to take. The pastor begins to rely on these committed laborers who support the church physically, spiritually and financially.

But some of these dedicated workers stop working long enough to look around at members who are doing nothing. They wonder if they are regarded as "The Drudge." When there is work to be done, they are the first ones that are called upon, while the others sit idly by. They are seldom even thanked. Their hearts fill with resentment and they suddenly feel very tired.

A recliner and the remote look extremely inviting. "Family time" suddenly becomes vitally important. The boat, the golf course, and relaxation—anything and everything begins to look more appealing than working in the church!

The worker doesn't know quite how to handle the situation. He can't admit the truth to the pastor and congregation, or even to himself.

The truth would be, "You expect me to do all the work, while most of you do nothing. So I quit. I have decided to backslide with the rest of you."

Since he can't do that, he leaves the church. People ask him why he left. He can't reveal his real reason for leaving. His only solution is to point his accusing finger toward the pastor. He surely did or said something wrong. He can blame him! (This is a tactic as old as the Garden of Eden. "Eve made me do it!" "The devil made me do it!") Now it is, "The bad pastor made me do it!" He finds another church where he can slip in, sit for an hour on Sunday morning, and be appreciated for just showing up. He has left the pastor with his remaining congregation, now looking at him a little more skeptically, wondering if the accusations they have heard about him are true.

And the pastor's pace becomes just a little slower—and the recliner and the boat look pretty appealing to him too.

Chapter 9

Don't Give Up

Thousands of pastors are giving up the fight. Thousands are not finishing their race.

Jesus warned us "...because iniquity shall abound, the love of many shall wax cold." *Matthew 24:12*

Sin surrounds us today, nearly crushing us. But the love that Christ placed in us for dying, hurting humanity does not have to turn to ice. We do not have to...

> Quit loving rebellious sheep.
> Quit loving sinners who need salvation.
> Quit loving sheep who cuddle hungry wolves.
> Begin to love ourselves more than our sheep.

Jesus said, "...the good shepherd giveth his life for the sheep." *John 10:11*

The good shepherd gives his time, strength, love, forgiveness, and *even his reputation.*

Lies destroy our reputations. If a pastor expects to have a distinguished reputation and be looked up to and respected by all, he has not read the Bible!

The Bible instructs us to "Let this mind be in you,

which was also in Christ Jesus: Who...*made himself of no reputation*." *Philippians 2:7*

Jesus was called mad, devil-possessed, a liar, a law-breaker and a blasphemer.

>Some **told** lies about Jesus.
>
>And some **believed** lies about Jesus.
>
>There are always tongues willing to **tell** lies.
>
>And there are always ears willing to **listen to** lies.

Unfortunately, there are always waiting ears, anxious to hear and ready to believe every lie that is told about a pastor.

(If we believed even half the lies that were told about us, we would not be able to live with ourselves.)

Jesus said, "Blessed are ye, when men shall revile you, and persecute you, and shall *say all manner of evil against you falsely*, for my sake. *Rejoice, and be exceeding glad*: for great is your reward in heaven: for so persecuted they the prophets which were before you." *Matthew 5:11-12*

It is hard to feel blessed when we are lied about. It is extremely hard to rejoice during these times. And it is nearly impossible to be glad—not just glad—but **exceeding** glad when we hear the lies being told about us.

Exceeding glad means: **Really glad! Very glad! Extremely glad!**

People lied about God's messengers before our time, and people will lie about us. There is only one way to stay happy in the midst of this. "Rejoice, and be exceeding glad: *for great is your reward in heaven....*" *Matthew 5:12*

Our reward is:

Not now. It comes later.
Not here. We receive it in heaven.

We must keep our hearts in heaven and our eyes on Jesus! Paul told us we must keep looking to Jesus to keep going.

"**Looking unto Jesus the author and finisher of our faith**; who for the joy that was set before him endured the cross, despising the shame, and is set down at the right hand of the throne of God. For **consider him** that endured such contradiction of sinners against himself, lest **ye be wearied and faint in your minds**." *Hebrews 12:2-3*

Do you see what happens if we quit looking at Jesus? Our minds will faint! We will quit! We will fall away! We will depart from the faith!

"Whatsoever ye do, do it heartily, **as to the Lord**, and not unto men; knowing that of the Lord ye shall receive the reward of the inheritance: for **ye serve the Lord Christ**." *Colossians 3:23-24*

Don't Fall!

"A thousand shall fall at thy side, and ten thousand at thy right hand; but it shall not come nigh thee." *Psalm 91:7*

Eighteen thousand pastors may walk away from the call of God every year, but _you_ don't have to be in the crowd!

"Let no man deceive you by any means: for that day shall not come, except there come *a falling away* first...." *II Thessalonians 2:3*

Have you already fallen? Then get back up! We need you! The harvest is ripe! The laborers are few! "For a just man falleth seven times, and riseth up again...." *Proverbs 24:16*

Don't Depart!

"Now the Spirit speaketh expressly, that in the latter times *some shall depart* from the faith, giving heed to seducing spirits, and doctrines of devils." *I Timothy 4:1*

Yes, some are departing from the faith. But you don't have to be one who walks away from your faith in God and His call on your life!

Press On!

Paul wrote: "I *press* toward the mark for the prize of the high calling of God in Christ Jesus." *Philippians 3:14*

Pressing on means to keep on going, even though pressure bombards us! Many are quitting under the pressures of the ministry. You don't have to be one!

Keep Running!

"Wherefore seeing we also are compassed about with so great a cloud of witnesses, let us lay aside every weight, and the sin which doth so easily beset us, and **let us run** with patience the race that is set before us." *Hebrews 12:1*

Take off the weights. Get rid of the sins. Run!

Don't Faint!

"And let us not be weary in well doing: for in due season we shall reap, if we faint not." *Galatians 6:9*

Don't faint! We need you!

Do you think you are not needed? We hear many pastors refer to their "small churches." As a God-ordained pastor, you are part of a blood-bought eternal church.

It was founded by our Lord Jesus Christ.

The gates of hell itself will not prevail against God's triumphant church!

It is a victorious church!

It has endured an onslaught from the hosts of darkness for twenty centuries!

Yet God's church continues to win souls, evangelize nations, feed the hungry, minister to the imprisoned, clothe the naked, visit the sick, care for the widows and orphans, and raise a standard of righteousness in the world. The devil and the world despise our standard of righteousness, but we continue to fight, armed with God's Word, our sword.

The devil would like nothing more than to stop **every word** from **every mouth** of **every servant** of the living God.

The Word of God is the sword that God has placed in the hand of His church. It is spoken by the messengers of God. It is our only weapon. We can't let Satan disarm us! We must fight for Jesus Christ, our righteous King, even unto death.

"For...it pleased God by the foolishness of **preaching** to save them that believe." *I Corinthians 1:21*

You are a pastor of the church founded by Jesus Christ! Jesus was sent from heaven to found this church! Jesus purchased this church with His own blood! Jesus is returning to earth to receive this church into heaven! He has made **you** a pastor of this great church! **Your work** is vital!

Churches held in homes were mentioned in the Bible. They were never identified as small churches! Here are three:

1. "Aquila and Priscilla salute you much in the Lord, with the church **that is in their house.**" *I Corinthians 16:19*

2. "And to our beloved Apphia, and Archippus our fellowsoldier, and **to the church in thy house.**" *Philemon 1:2*

3. "Salute the brethren which are in Laodicea, and Nymphas, **and the church which is in his house.**" *Colossians 4:15*

The Bible does not refer to little churches, medium churches and mega churches! We are all part of that glorious church that Christ loved and died for. Every pastor, no matter the size of his flock or the capacity of his sheep shed, is needed to do the work of our Lord.

- There were only 120 men and women in the upper room.

- The reformation began as Martin Luther taught just a few students at Wittenberg.

- John Wesley found Christ at a back alley prayer meeting at Aldersgate.

- Charles H. Spurgeon joined the race in a tiny chapel.

- Jesus chose twelve disciples to follow Him.

- Jesus appeared to a crowd of five hundred after His resurrection, but only one hundred twenty showed up to wait for His promise to send the Holy Spirit upon them.

- Noah faithfully warned his generation, but salvaged only his family from God's judgment.

- Peter described Lot as a righteous man who was daily vexed with seeing and hearing the filthy lifestyle and conversation. Yet he didn't even save his whole family. Only two corrupt daughters were salvaged.

Don't judge your worth by the size of your congregation!

Don't judge your worth by the grumbling and murmuring of your congregation!

Judge your worth by your obedience to the voice of your King!

If you faithfully pastor a flock in your house, you are fulfilling your calling. Our job is not to fill pews with people. ***Our ministry is to fill people with God!*** If every pastor simply remains faithful to the flock God has given to him to pastor, this job will get done!

Chapter 10

Crucial Days

This is not a day to give in to discouragement. We are living in perilous times. Every God-ordained voice needs to be heard in this crucial day.

> Families are broken.
> Children are neglected.
> Minds are perverted.
> The Bible is ridiculed.
> Churches are locked on Sunday evenings.
> The name of Jesus is blasphemed.
> Prayer is outlawed.
> The Ten Commandments are ripped off walls.
> Sunday Schools are closing.
> Violence is increasing.
> Sodomy is accepted.

This is the day we were warned about: "Let us consider one another to provoke unto love and to good works: not forsaking the assembling of ourselves together, as the manner of some is; but exhorting one another: and **_so much the more_**, as ye see the day approaching." *Hebrews 10:24-25*

Unfortunately, the church is not meeting **_more_** as we see the day of Christ's return approaching. It is meeting **_less!_**

Pastor, if you are born-again, blood-bought and God-called—we need you! Don't give up! If a church member has attacked you, remember what Paul did when the viper attacked him. He shook it off! The islanders and 275 men from his ship watched, waiting for Paul to swell up and die. He didn't. He did what we need to do. We need to shake off the serpent and go on about God's business. The parishioners will eventually come to their senses and realize we are not going to swell up and die.

There will always be the Jezebels trying to kill the Elijahs. Rather than letting them destroy us, we need to look at their endings.

Jezebel was torn apart by dogs.

Elijah was picked up in a chariot of fire and ushered into heaven in style.

Jezebels have one purpose in mind—to kill the man of God. Oh, today's Jezebel may not gather up assassins to kill him. Today's Jezebels will most likely not even threaten the pastor to his face. But the spirit will be the same—and the purpose will be the same—to kill the ministry and stop the words of God's messenger. **_Don't let them do it._**

When we feel the pressure closing in around us, we need to pray the prayer Uncle Bud Robinson prayed:

"Oh, Lord, give me a back-bone as big as a saw log, and ribs like the sleepers under the church floor; put iron shoes on me, and galvanized breeches. And give me a rhinoceros hide for a skin, and hang a wagon load of determination up in the gable-end of my soul, and help me to sign the contract to fight the devil as long as I've got a fist, and bite him as long as I've got a tooth and then gum him till I die. All this I ask for Christ's sake, AMEN!"

You may have to flee from one place and settle in another, but continue to proclaim the Word of the Lord wherever you land.

It's no shame to flee from persecutors. Jesus escaped from angry mobs. Paul was let down a wall in a basket by the disciples to escape his persecutors. The early Christians fled from Jerusalem. Elijah fled from Jezebel and her team of hit men. But each one of them kept speaking the Word of the Lord. Not one threw away his sword and retreated from the battle.

We need every voice who will fearlessly speak the Word of God. We must show "to the generation to come the praises of the LORD, and his strength, and his wonderful works that he hath done." *Psalm 78:4*

Will we allow our voices to be silenced by the enemy of the gospel?

Dare we risk hearing our world cry, "The harvest is past, the summer is ended, and we are not saved." *Jeremiah 8:20*

Chapter 11

May God Strengthen Your Heart

When people attack a shepherd, his heart is smitten and wounded.

David wrote: "My heart is smitten, and withered like grass. My heart is wounded within me." *Psalm 102:4, 109:22*

Don't be disheartened because of your persecutors.

Would you rather be the liar, or the lied about?

Would you rather be the persecutor, or the persecuted?

Would you rather be the slapper, or the slapped?

Which would you rather hear Jesus say? "Depart from me, ye that work iniquity," or "Well done, thou good and faithful servant!"

God's Marching Orders

Here are the marching orders for God's ministers: "I charge thee therefore before God, and the Lord Jesus Christ, who shall judge the quick and the dead at his appearing and his kingdom;"

"Preach the word; be instant in season, out of season; reprove, rebuke, exhort with all longsuffering and doctrine."

"For the time will come when they will not endure sound doctrine; but after their own lusts shall they heap to themselves teachers, having itching ears; and they shall turn away their ears from the truth, and shall be turned unto fables."

"But watch thou in all things, endure afflictions, do the work of an evangelist, make full proof of thy ministry." *II Timothy 4:1-5*

Follow Jesus! He said, "I have glorified thee on the earth: ***I have finished the work which thou gavest me to do.***" *John 17:4*

Don't just ***begin*** your work! ***Finish it!***

Chapter 12

Leave the Results to God

The **_works_** of your ministry are up to you.

The **_results_** of your ministry are up to the Lord.

God called Ezekiel to speak His Word. It was up to him to speak for God whether anyone listened or not. God warned him when He sent him to the crowds that no one would listen to him. Because Ezekiel was faithful, those who listened to his message will be without excuse on their day of judgment.

God sent Ezekiel into the ministry with these words: "Son of man, I send thee to the children of Israel, to a rebellious nation that hath rebelled against me: they and their fathers have transgressed against me, even unto this very day. For they are impudent children and stiffhearted. I do send thee unto them; and thou shalt say unto them. Thus saith the Lord GOD."

"And they, **_whether they will hear, or whether they will forbear_**, (for they are a rebellious house,) **_yet shall know that there hath been a prophet among them._**"

"And thou, son of man, be not afraid of them, neither be afraid of their words, though briers and thorns be with

77

thee, and thou dost dwell among scorpions: be not afraid of their words, nor be dismayed at their looks, though they be a rebellious house.   And **thou shalt speak my words unto them, whether they will hear, or whether they will forbear**: for they are most rebellious. But thou, son of man, hear what I say unto thee; **be not thou rebellious** like that rebellious house: **open thy mouth**, and eat that I give thee." *Ezekiel 2:3-8*

Having a rebellious congregation gives a pastor no excuse to become a rebellious messenger. Our responsibility is to speak the Word of the Lord, whether or not anyone chooses to listen and obey it.

God called Jeremiah with this command: "Thou therefore gird up thy loins, and arise, and speak unto them all that I command thee: be not dismayed at their faces, lest I confound thee before them.

"For, behold, I have made thee this day a defenced city, and an iron pillar, and brazen walls...and **they shall fight against thee**; but **they shall not prevail** against thee; for I am with thee, saith the LORD, to deliver thee." *Jeremiah 1:17-19*

Who would fight against Jeremiah as he preached? Unfortunately, it was Israel, the people chosen by God— the congregation God gave to Jeremiah.

The very sheep God calls us to shepherd may be the ones who fight against us. But even that is no excuse to give up.

Chapter 13

A Word of Warning

The devil cannot stand it when God's messengers are praised. On the heels of every victory is a battle.

Jesus was surrounded by people praising Him on Palm Sunday. *On Friday, they were calling for His execution.*

Elijah prayed fire down from heaven and the people worshiped God. The false prophets were destroyed. *Jezebel got the news, called for his head, and Elijah ran for his life.*

Moses held his rod over the sea, and the waters were parted. The enemy was overthrown. The Israelites rejoiced, praised, shouted, and danced. *Three days later they needed water and accused Moses of bringing them into the desert to kill them all of thirst.*

David killed Goliath. The women sang: "Saul hath slain his thousands, and David his ten thousands!" *King Saul hurled his javelin at David, hoping to pin him to the wall with it.*

Paul was on a ship going down. An angel appeared with a message. Paul gave orders and all 276 men were saved. They swam and floated to an island where the natives received them with kindness. ***The island was crowded with the 276 men from the ship and all the natives. A viper chose to attach itself to just one man…the apostle Paul.***

When you are being praised—brace yourself. The enemy will be waiting for his opportunity. Be armed, prayed up, and ready for him.

"The devil is come down **unto you**, having great wrath, because he knoweth that he hath but a short time. Submit yourselves therefore to God. Resist the devil, and he will flee from you." *Revelation 12:12; James 4:7*

Toughen Up!

Paul wrote about how we must be when times get tough: "Finally, my brethren, **be strong** in the Lord, and in the power of his might. Therefore, my beloved brethren, be ye steadfast (tough), unmovable, always abounding in the work of the Lord, forasmuch as ye know that your labour is not in vain in the Lord." *Ephesians 6:10; I Corinthians 15:58*

Abide!

During our times of discouragement and temptation to quit, God has often reminded us of "our special verse." It is our call to tough it out in the hard times. It is found in an unlikely place—nestled in the Christmas story. Here it is:

"And there were in the same country shepherds **abiding** in the field, **keeping watch over their flock by night**." *Luke 2:8*

> It is nighttime.
> The world is growing darker by the minute.
> Wolves abound.
> Danger lurks.
> God's precious sheep are vulnerable.

Shepherds need to **abide** in the field, keeping watch over the flocks that our great Shepherd has entrusted to our care. Abide means to **remain; stay; persevere; or endure**.

Jesus left the splendors of heaven to come down to a perverted, faithless human race. Thank God He **stayed** until His work was done. His cry yet echoes from Calvary's hill: **"It is finished."**

Abraham, referred to in the New Testament as a faithful man, the father of us all, was promised a land for his descendants. When he died, he held title to only one small piece of land—a burial plot for his beloved wife. **Yet today**—today Abraham's descendants possess the Promised Land!

"For all the promises of God in him are yea, and in him Amen, unto the glory of God by us." *II Corinthians 1:20*

"For the vision is yet for an appointed time, but at the end it shall speak, and not lie: though it tarry, wait for it; because it will surely come, it will not tarry." *Habakkuk 2:3*

> What God said, He has done.
> What God says, He will do.

Hold on to your faith!

Hold on to your calling!

Finish the work God has given you to do!

Paul kept the faith, even as he wrote from his prison cell to the church he longed to be with: "But I trust in the Lord Jesus to send Timotheus shortly unto you, that I also may be of good comfort, when I know your state. For I **have no man likeminded**, who will naturally care for your state. For **all seek their own**, not the things which are Jesus Christ's." *Philippians 2:19-21*

Paul, called by God to do a mighty work, a powerful teacher of the Word of God, looked at his self-centered leaders, and wrote from his jail cell: "At least I have Timothy."

Moses stood by, as God killed a good portion of his congregation because of their rebellion. The same congregation, who had walked across dry land in the middle of the Red Sea, ate food delivered to them from heaven and drank water from a rock that became a river...now murmured...and complained...and moaned...and rebelled... and doubted...and grumbled.

Through it all, God expects us to remain with our flocks. God refers to His pastors as gifts to His church. (Few on earth will refer to their pastor as a gift—but it is God's favor we seek, not man's!)

"Wherefore he saith, When he ascended up on high, he led captivity captive, and **_gave gifts_** unto men...and **_he gave_** *some, apostles; and some, prophets; and some, evangelists; and some, pastors and teachers*; for the perfecting of the saints, for the work of the ministry, for the edifying of the body of Christ: till we all come in the unity of the faith, and of the knowledge of the Son of God, unto a perfect man, unto the measure of the stature of the fullness of Christ." *Ephesians 4:8-13*

God told the Israelites: "And I, behold, I have taken your brethren the Levites from among the children of Israel: **to you they are given as a gift** for the LORD, to do the service of the tabernacle of the congregation." *Numbers 18:6*

Jesus left a message to each of the seven churches in the book of Revelation. He delivered it through His beloved disciple, John. Listen to the way he addressed each message:

1. "Unto the angel of the church of Ephesus...."
2. "Unto the angel of the church in Smyrna...."
3. "To the angel of the church in Pergamos...."
4. "Unto the angel of the church in Thyatira...."
5. "Unto the angel of the church in Sardis...."
6. "To the angel of the church in Philadelphia...."
7. "Unto the angel of the church of Laodicea...."

To the angel...to <u>my messenger</u>...to <u>the shepherd</u> in My church who leads My flock....

How can we let discouragement overtake our joy when we serve such a Master? His grace is so amazing that He refers to His messengers as **gifts** to His church! His mercy is so awesome that He refers to the pastors of the seven churches as His angels (messengers)! His love is so wonderful that no other opinions should matter to us in the least!

Chapter 14

The Encouragers

We have dwelt on the discouraging times in these pages and neglected the glorious and rewarding times of the ministry for one reason. This is a book written to encourage pastors who are tempted to quit the ministry. It is the discouragements, the disappointments, the complainers, the betrayers, and the haters that the enemy uses to wear us down.

When Moses turned the reigns of his ministry over to young Joshua, he asked the congregation to encourage him and strengthen him. In nearly every congregation there are the helpers; the strengtheners; the thankful; the cheerful; the encouragers; those who love us in spite of us. There are the Aarons and the Hurs who hold up the hands of Moses in the heat of the battle.

How is it that the grumblers stand out in a crowd, while the encouragers just fade into the background during the rough times? Could it be we pastors are guilty of focusing on the wrong thing? What do you see in this picture?

Is your answer, "A black dot"? We often look at the one black dot, rather than all the white that surrounds it.

Jesus ministered in the midst of a mob who screamed for His death, tried to push Him over a cliff, gathered rocks to stone Him, called Him a liar and a blasphemer, accused Him of being devil-possessed, pronounced Him insane and finally succeeded in nailing Him to a cross.

Why did He continue?

"Looking unto Jesus the author and finisher of our faith; who **_for the joy that was set before him_** endured...." *Hebrews 12:2*

He focused on the joy that was set before Him....

"Take heed therefore unto yourselves, and to all **_the flock_**, over the which the Holy Ghost hath made you overseers, to feed the church of God, which **_he hath purchased with his own blood._**" *Acts 20:28*

"I am the good shepherd: the good shepherd giveth his life for the sheep." *John 10:11*

Jesus endured because He was purchasing His flock, the church, His beloved bride....

"And I, John, saw the holy city, new Jerusalem, coming down from God out of heaven, prepared **_as a bride adorned for her husband_**. And I heard a great voice out of heaven saying, Behold, the tabernacle of God is with men, and he will dwell with them, and they shall be his people, and God himself shall be with them, and be their God. And God shall wipe away all tears from their eyes; and there shall be no more death, neither sorrow, nor crying, neither shall there be any more pain: for the former things are passed away.

And he that sat upon the throne said, Behold, I make all things new. And he said unto me, Write: for these words are true and faithful." *Revelation 21:2-5*

The bride, loved by our King so much that He purchased her with His own blood, was ***the joy*** that was set before Him. And for the JOY that was set before Him, Christ endured.

In Light of Eternity

A man lived a life of wealth and health for 70 years. His days were filled with loyal friends, constant love and joy. As he neared death, his friends and family gathered around him. They were shocked to hear this bitter complaint pour from his dying body.

"I have had seventy wonderful years—except for eight hours one dark day. I suffered a bad headache. My neighbor was rude to me. My dog snarled at me. My wife refused to greet me with a smile when she brought my breakfast. My son was disobedient and rebellious."

The man's final words were full of resentment. "Those eight hours of my life were dreadful."

It would be utterly ridiculous for a man to complain about having troubles for eight hours of his life and forget about the 613,192 hours he was trouble free!

Let us consider this story in the light of eternity.

We will liken the eight hours of trouble to our lifetime on earth.

If trials and troubles fill our entire lifetime, what is that, in comparison to eternity?

Will we spend our first 10,000 years in heaven, complaining bitterly: "I had trouble while I was living on earth. People didn't like me. Some even told lies about me. I was slandered."

Doesn't it strike you as ridiculous that we ungrateful people dare to complain about troubles in our life when we are promised **ETERNITY** trouble free?

"For what is your life? It is even a vapour, that appeareth for a little time, and then vanisheth away." *James 4:14*

No wonder the apostle Paul could say, "But what things were gain to me, those I counted loss for Christ. Yea doubtless, and I count all things but loss for the excellency of the knowledge of Christ Jesus my Lord: for whom I have suffered the loss of all things, and do count them but dung, that I may win Christ." *Philippians 3:7-8*

Those Miserable Black Dots

There will be no black dot to mar the bride when all our work is finished.

Today the black dots are visible. They are not only visible to us; they are also visible to God.

Listen, as God describes the spots and blemishes: "The Lord knoweth how to deliver the godly out of temptations, and to reserve the unjust unto the day of judgment to be punished: but chiefly them that walk after the flesh in the lust of uncleanness, and despise government. Presumptuous **(arrogant)** are they, self-willed, they are not afraid to speak evil of dignities.

"Whereas angels, which are greater in power and might, bring not railing accusation against them before the Lord. But these, as natural brute beasts, made to be taken and destroyed, speak evil of the things that they understand not; and shall utterly perish in their own corruption; and shall receive the reward of unrighteousness, as they that count it pleasure to riot in the day time.

"Spots they are and blemishes, sporting themselves with their own deceivings *while they feast with you."* II *Peter 2:10-13*

The spots and blemishes may feast with the church today. However, no spot or blemish will enter heaven.

"...Christ also loved the church, and gave himself for it; that he might sanctify and cleanse it with the washing of water by the word, that he might present it to himself a glorious church, **not having spot**, or wrinkle, or any such thing; but that it should be holy and **without blemish**." *Ephesians 5:25-27*

Jesus will receive His church into heaven, and it will be a glorious church.

The spots that show up so clearly today will be absent tomorrow.

God left us this glimpse of heaven:

"And a voice came out of the throne, saying, Praise our God, all ye his servants, and ye that fear him, both small and great. And I heard as it were the voice of a great multitude, and as the voice of many waters, and as the voice of mighty thunderings, saying, Alleluia: for the Lord God omnipotent reigneth."

"Let us be glad and rejoice, and give honour to him: for the marriage of the Lamb is come, and his wife hath made herself ready. And to her was granted that she should be arrayed in fine linen, clean and white: for the fine linen is the righteousness of saints. And he saith unto me, Write, blessed are they which are called unto the marriage supper of the Lamb. And he saith unto me, These are the true sayings of God." *Revelation 19:5-9*

Until that glorious day, we must continue to heed our Lord's words to us: "Watchman, what of the night? Watchman, what of the night?" *Isaiah 21:11*

Let us answer our Lord with this renewed commitment: "I must work the works of him that sent me, while it is day: the night cometh, when no man can work." *John 9:4*

Let us remember the blessings reserved for the faithful shepherds who stayed with their flock during the night hours that first Christmas.

The angel of the Lord came upon them!
The glory of the Lord shone round about them!
They heard God's choir in the skies!
They looked upon Jesus!

"Let the LORD, the God of the spirits of all flesh, set a man over the congregation, which may go out before them, and which may go in before them, and which may lead them out, and which may bring them in; that the congregation of the LORD be not as sheep which have no shepherd." Numbers 27:16-17

I Climbed the Mountain

The night was black
Rain was pelting the mountain
Where the little lamb lay.
I looked up just as
A flashing spear of lightning
Lit the night sky.

And I saw the Shepherd,
Balancing on a ledge,
Holding onto a branch with one hand,
Reaching down with the other.
Just a quick glimpse,
And the light was gone.

Darkness seemed especially black
Until the next flash revealed the lamb.
Its head was buried in its wool
And it was trembling,
Aware only of its own misery,
the Shepherd unheeded.

Thunders crashed through the mountains.
I waited anxiously to see the next scene.
But then I saw the Shepherd.
And I trembled. His eyes no longer
Looked upon the lamb.
They were fixed on me.

I knew instantly what He
Expected me to do.
Me! I was no mountain climber!
The mountain was huge, menacing.
I trembled with fear
Just thinking about the climb!
Failure would mean my doom!

Even in darkness I could feel His eyes—
Boring into my own.
I could not remain a spectator.
He was forcing me
To become part of the scene.

I vibrated with dread.
How dare He force me
To get involved?
The sheerness of the mountain wall;
Raging winds, deafening thunder;
Streaks of lightning—I was terrified!

Must I sacrifice myself…
Just for a little lamb?
Didn't this Shepherd have enough lambs
Safely at home in His fold?
Why should I risk my life
On such a night as this?

The next flash of light
Revealed what I already knew.
His eyes were still piercing mine.

He was not going to let me
View this scene in peace.
I cautiously began to climb.

Grabbing a branch.
Waiting for the light to flash.
Finding a toehold here,
And a stepping stone there.
I got about halfway up
When I decided to quit.

I looked down only to see
That I couldn't descend.
I had no place to go.
So I just kept climbing.
Taking one small step at a time,
I at last reached the cowering lamb.

The Shepherd's hand was just above it.
It only took a small effort on my part
To span that small space between
The Shepherd's hand and His little lamb.
I watched as the lamb was safely
Cuddled to the heart of its Shepherd.

I heard the faint bleat of another lamb—
And another. Then another.
Wounded lambs. Lost lambs.
Dying lambs. Shivering lambs.
I forgot my fears, as I handed them up
To their waiting Shepherd.

93

He took each one tenderly.
Caressing, covering, warming them
In the folds of His garment.
I passed another to Him.
Watching and waiting to see
Him nestle it to Himself.

But I saw instead the Shepherd's face,
The sun had never shone as brightly.
He was smiling—smiling at me!
I felt myself being lifted then
Straight into the Shepherd's bosom,
Enfolded right next to His heart.

Nestled beside me were rescued lambs,
Quiet now, contented and safe.
The Shepherd spoke gently to me:
"Well done, My child! Well done!
You are a good and faithful servant.
Enter thou into the joy of the Lord."

Eternal Joy.
The Rescued Lambs.
The Smiling Shepherd.
The Everlasting Day.
The Forgotten Night.

I am so glad
I climbed the mountain!

CAROLYN WILDE

Chapter 15

Dwight L. Moody Deals With a Critic

Note: Everyone who serves God has his share of critics. Every decision is questioned, every comment is scrutinized, and every expression is examined. There is only one way to keep from getting criticized by the critics. Do nothing. As long as you are doing anything for our Master, you are subjecting yourself to opposition, criticism, hostility, hatred and rejection. Here is how Dwight L. Moody, one of the world's most successful evangelists, dealt with one of his critics.

By the time Dwight was 17, he had become a successful shoe salesman for Holton's Shoe Store. Moody accepted Christ in the back room of the shoe store through the guidance of his Sunday School teacher. Later, he became actively involved in the Plymouth Congregational Church in Chicago. As a layman, he began renting the church pews and filling them up with men and women whom he had invited.

He went on to become one of the world's greatest evangelists. But he never got away from his simple commitment and the memories of the first time he stood up to speak as a young man, when one of the deacons assured him that, in his opinion, he would serve God best by keeping still. Another critic praised Moody for his zeal but pleaded with him, saying that he should realize his limitations and not attempt to speak in public. "You make too many mistakes in grammar."

Moody patiently replied: "I know I make mistakes, and I lack many things, but I'm doing the best I can with what I've got." He then quietly looked at the man and searchingly inquired, "Look here, friend, you've got grammar enough. What are you doing with it for the Master?"

John Wesley's Shout of Relief

John Wesley wrote over 200 books, edited a magazine, compiled dictionaries in four languages, and composed a home medical handbook—all in his own handwriting! He traveled over 250,000 miles on horseback—the equivalent of riding ten times around the world along its equator. He preached more than 40,000 powerful sermons, some to crowds of over 20,000. Only eternity will reveal how many hundreds of thousands of souls were saved through John's committed life.

He was constantly heckled and jeered. He was riding along a dusty road one day when it occurred to him that three whole days had passed in which he had suffered no persecution! He was horrified. No bricks had been thrown. He had not even been bombarded with one egg!

He knew he was in trouble. He immediately stopped his horse with a shout and fell to his knees.

"My Lord," he cried. "Show me my fault! Am I backslidden? Have I sinned?"

A fellow on the other side of the hedge heard his prayer and recognized him.

"I'll fix that Methodist preacher," he said, picking up a brick and hurling it at him.

The brick fell short of its mark, but John, leaping to his feet, joyfully shouted, "Thank God! It's all right! I still have God's presence!"

George Whitefield's Consolation

George Whitefield, sometimes referred to as "The Lightning Rod of the Great Awakening" wrote these words in his journal:

"At present I can rejoice in being deserted by one and used unkind by another, who at the great day must own me to be their spiritual father."

The 6 Words of William Borden

In 1904 William Borden graduated from a Chicago high school. As heir to the Borden Dairy estate, he was already a millionaire. For his high school graduation present, his parents gave him a trip around the world. Traveling through Asia, the Middle East, and Europe, Borden felt a growing burden for the world's hurting people. Finally, he wrote home to say, "I am going to give my life to prepare for the mission field." After making this decision, William Borden wrote two words in the back of his Bible: **"No Reserves."**

Borden arrived at Yale University in 1905 as just one more freshman. Very quickly, however, Borden's classmates noticed something unusual about him. One of them wrote: "He came to college far ahead, spiritually, of any of us. He had already given his heart in full surrender to Christ and had really done it. We who were his classmates learned to lean on him and find in him a strength that was solid as a rock, just because of this settled purpose and consecration."

Borden's first disappointment was hearing Yale's president speak on the students' need of "having a fixed purpose." After that speech Borden wrote: "He neglected to say what our purpose should be, and where we should get the ability to persevere and the strength to resist temptations."

As Borden looked at his fellow students, he lamented that the results of this empty philosophy were moral weakness and sin-ruined lives.

During his first semester at Yale, Borden started a movement that transformed the campus. A friend described it: "It was well on in the first term when Bill and I began to pray together in the morning before breakfast. We had been meeting only a short time when a third student joined us and soon after, a fourth. The time was spent in prayer after a brief reading of Scripture. Bill's handling of Scripture was helpful. He would read to us from the Bible, show us something that God had promised and then claim the promise with assurance."

Borden's group was the beginning of the daily groups of prayer that spread to every one of the college classes. By the end of his first year, 150 freshman were meeting for weekly Bible studies. By the time he was a senior, 1,000 out of Yale's 1,300 students were meeting in such groups. Borden made it his habit to choose the most "incorrigible" students and try to bring them to salvation.

"In his sophomore year, we organized Bible study groups and divided up the class of 300 or more, each man taking a certain number, so that all might, if possible, be reached for Christ. The names were gone over one by one, and the question asked, 'Who will take this person or that?' When it came to one who was a hard proposition, there would be an ominous pause. Nobody wanted the responsibility. Then Bill's voice would be heard. 'Put him down to me.'"

Borden did not confine his ministry outreach to the Yale campus. He rescued drunks on the streets of New Haven. To rehabilitate them, he founded the Yale Hope Mission. He was often found in the lower parts of the city at night, on the street, in a cheap lodging house or in some restaurant to which he had taken a poor hungry fellow to feed him, seeking to lead one more to Christ.

Borden's missionary call came to focus on Muslims in China. He never wavered from that goal. William inspired his classmates to consider missionary service. One of them said: "He certainly was one of the strongest characters I have ever known, and he put backbone into the rest of us at college. There was real iron in him, and I always felt he was of the stuff martyrs were made of. Although he was a millionaire, Bill realized always that he must be about his Father's business. He had no time to waste in the pursuit of amusement."

Although Borden refused to join a fraternity, he did more with his classmates in his senior year than ever before. He presided over the huge student missionary conference held at Yale and served as president of the honor society, Phi Beta Kappa. Upon graduation from Yale, Borden turned down some high paying job offers.

He also wrote two more words in his Bible: **"NO RETREATS."**

He went on to graduate work at Princeton Seminary in New Jersey. When he finished his studies at Princeton, Borden sailed for China. He stopped first in Egypt to study Arabic, so he could work with Muslims. While in Egypt, Bill came down with spinal meningitis. Within a month, 25-year-old William Borden was dead.

When the death of William Whiting Borden was cabled from Egypt, it seemed as though a wave of sorrow went round the world. Borden not only had given away his wealth, but also himself, in a way so joyous and natural that he made it seem like a privilege rather than a sacrifice.

A waste, you say? Not in God's plan. Prior to his death Borden had written two more words in his Bible. Underneath the first four words he had written, he had penned his final two words.

1. **NO RESERVES.**
2. **NO RETREATS.**
3. **NO REGRETS.**

Chapter 16

Pastors, Prepare Your People!

There is an end-day, mighty army prophesied by Joel. This is how the Bible describes the soldiers in this army: "They shall run like mighty men; they shall climb the wall like men of war; and they shall march every one on his ways, and they shall not break their ranks: neither shall one thrust another; they shall walk every one in his path...." *Joel 2:7-8*

If you look closely, you will see this army forming today. It is beginning with pastors. There is not one among us who has not suffered hurt, betrayal, and rejection. As a result, we have entered, one by one, into a closer fellowship with Jesus and His body.

Paul wrote about this: "That I may know him, and the power of his resurrection, and the fellowship of his sufferings, being made conformable unto his death." *Philippians 3:10*

"The fellowship of his sufferings...."

There is fellowship among those who have shared suffering. Soldiers who have battled the enemy have a special comradeship.

Cancer survivors have a bond with one another.

The firemen who battled the raging inferno left behind by terrorists on September 11, 2001, have a kinship that is shared by no outsider.

Pastors also have a special relationship today that they did not have in the past. Pastors are praying for and building one another up, rather than tearing one another down. They are encouraging one another to hold on. They have entered into what Paul wrote as "the fellowship of his sufferings."

We see increased persecution and intense pressure building up against those who fearlessly proclaim the Word of God.

This assault will not come only against pastors.

This assault will soon be unleashed against the sheep.

The lies, slanders, criticisms, attacks, hatred, and even death threats that have bombarded God's messengers will soon extend to all the people of God.

The sheep of God's flock are going to be viciously attacked by the enemies of righteousness.

If pastors are finding it hard to endure, what will happen to God's sheep?

"If thou hast run with the footmen, and they have wearied thee, then how canst thou contend with horses? And if in the land of peace, wherein thou trustedst, they wearied thee, then how wilt thou do in the swelling of Jordan?" *Jeremiah 12:5*

We must first toughen up ourselves. Then we can

prepare God's people for the persecution to come.

"Go through, go through the gates; prepare ye the way of the people; cast up, cast up the highway; gather out the stones; lift up a standard for the people. Behold, the LORD hath proclaimed unto the end of the world, Say ye to the daughter of Zion, Behold, thy salvation cometh; behold, his reward is with him, and his work before him. And they shall call them, the holy people, the redeemed of the LORD: and thou shalt be called, Sought out, A city not forsaken." *Isaiah 62:10-12*

"For if the trumpet give an uncertain sound, who shall prepare himself to the battle?" *I Corinthians 14:8*

"Feed the flock of God which is among you, taking the oversight thereof, not by constraint, but willingly; not for filthy lucre, but of a ready mind; neither as being lords over God's heritage, but being ensamples to the flock. And when the chief Shepherd shall appear, ye shall receive a crown of glory that fadeth not away." *I Peter 5:2-4*

"Blessed be God, even the Father of our Lord Jesus Christ, the Father of mercies, and the God of all comfort; Who comforteth us in all our tribulation, that we may be able to comfort them which are in any trouble, by the comfort wherewith we ourselves are comforted of God. For as the sufferings of Christ abound in us, so our consolation (comfort; sympathy) also aboundeth by Christ." *II Corinthians 1:3-5*

Pastors, we must leave an example of perseverance through trials to our sheep.

We must show them how to

> endure,
> hold fast,
> keep the faith,
> and cross the finish line.

If we can't do it, how can we expect more of them?

"Wherefore gird up the loins of your mind, be sober, and hope to the end for the grace that is to be brought unto you at the revelation of Jesus Christ." *I Peter 1:13*

"That good thing which was committed unto thee keep by the Holy Ghost which dwelleth in us." *II Timothy 1:14*

"...that which ye have already hold fast till I come." *Revelation 2:25*

"Behold, I come quickly: hold that fast which thou hast, that no man take thy crown." *Revelation 3:11*

Don't Soften God's Message!

Are you periodically tempted to soften God's message and thus soften your enemy's blows? Read the following poem prayerfully.

The Modernist Preacher Entering Hell

He was an ordained minister, but modern in his views,
He preached his doctrines to people in the pews.
He would not hurt their feelings, what'er the cost would be,
But for their smiles and friendship and compliments sought he.
His church was filled with wicked souls that should be saved from
    sin.
But never once he showed the way or tried a soul to win.
He preached about the lovely birds that twitter in the trees,
The babbling of the running brooks, the murm'ring of the seas.

He quoted fancy poetry that tickled list'ning ears;
When sorrow came to some, he tried to laugh away their tears.
His smooth and slippery sermons made the people slide to hell—
The harm he did by preaching goes beyond what we can tell.
He took our Holy Bible, and preached it full of holes,
The Virgin Birth, said he, can't be believed by honest souls.
The miracles of Jesus and the resurrection tale
For educated ones like us, today, cannot avail.

We're living in an age, said he, when wisdom rules and reigns.
When man's intelligence is great and superstition wanes.
He said, we're all God's children who live upon this earth,
No message of salvation, no need of second birth.
His coat was bought with money that he had wrongly gained.
For through his lying sermons his wealth he had obtained.
He was just like the soldiers that watched at Jesus' grave,
For money in abundance, to them, the people gave;
It all was theirs by telling what was a sinful lie—
A resurrected Savior, they too, were to deny.

The day at last had come for the minister to die,
When to his congregation he had to say good-bye.
His form lay cold and lifeless, his ministry was past,
His tongue with all its poison was hushed and stilled at last.
His funeral was grand, he was lauded to the skies—
They preached him into heaven where there are no good-byes.
Upon the lonely hill, underneath the shady trees,
His form was laid to rest in the whisp'ring of the breeze.

A tombstone was erected with the words: "He is at rest,
He's gone to heaven's glories to live among the blest."
His body now is lifeless, but Ah! His soul lives on,
He failed to enter in where they thought that he had gone.
The letters on the tombstone or that sermon some had heard,
Could not decide his destiny, 'twas not the final word.
He still had God to deal with, the one who knows the heart:
While others entered heaven, he heard the word, "Depart."

He pauses for a moment upon the brink of hell;
He stares into a depth where he evermore will dwell.
He hears the cries and groanings of souls he had misled.
He recognizes faces among the screaming dead.
He sees departed deacons which he once highly praised,
Their fingers pointing at him as they their voices raised:
"You stood behind the pulpit, and lived in awful sin,
We took you for a saint, but a serpent you have been."
Accusing cries! He hears them, "Ah! You have been to blame,
You led us into darkness when you were seeking fame."

"You preached your deadly poison, we thought you knew the
     way,

We fed you and we clothed you, we even raised your pay.
You've robbed us of a home where no teardrops ever flow.
Where days are always fair and the heav'nly breezes blow.
Where living streams are flowing, and saints and Angels sing,
Where every one is happy, and Hallelujahs ring.
We're in this place of torment, from which no soul returns;
We hear the cry of lost ones, we feel the sizzling burns;
Give us a drop of water, we're tortured in this flame;
You failed to preach salvation to us through Jesus' Name."

The preacher turns in horror, he tries to leave the scene,
He knows the awful future for every soul unclean,
But there he meets the devil, whom he had served so well,
He feels the demon powers, they drag him into hell.
Throughout eternal ages, his groans, too, must be heard—
He, too, must suffer torment—he failed to heed God's Word.
He feels God's wrath upon him, he hears the hot flames roar,
His doctrine now is different, he ridicules no more.

OSCAR C. ELIASON

Pastor, never soften the message to soften the blows.

Nineveh repented because Jonah grudgingly yielded to God's marching order: "Arise, go unto Nineveh, that great city, and *preach unto it the preaching that I bid thee." Jonah 3:2*

Jonah had concluded that going on a cruise would be a better use of his time and much more pleasurable than delivering God's ominous message to wicked people. As you know, Jonah finally landed on shore, picking seaweed from his bleached body.

He reluctantly began his three-day crusade with a blunt eight-word message from God: "Yet forty days, and Nineveh shall be overthrown."

Nineveh listened and repented.

Nineveh would not have repented if Jonah had not delivered God's message.

Certain judgment is awaiting every unrepentant sinner.

Sinners will not repent if God's spokesmen refuse to carry the eight-word message of Jesus: "Except ye repent, ye shall all likewise perish." (*Luke 13:3, 5*)

Never soften His message. Speak it clearly. The blows we receive are simply our battle scars. The war has already been won at Calvary. We are just carrying out the final commands of the Victor, while waiting for our King to arrive.

Fear Not

"Hearken unto me, ye that know righteousness, the people in whose heart is my law; ***fear ye not the reproach of men, neither be ye afraid of their revilings***. I have put my words in thy mouth, and I have covered thee in the shadow of mine hand...thou art my people." *Isaiah 51:7, 16*

"And daily in the temple, and in every house, ***they ceased not to teach and preach Jesus Christ***." *Acts 5:42*

Chapter 17

A Coming Storm Against the Church

Should it surprise us that the enemy rages against the church?

What hero of the Old or New Testaments had a life without battles? We are always at war! Timid voices recently counseled church leaders to eliminate all words in their teaching, preaching and writing that indicate that a spiritual war exists!

Do they realize how many words we would have to remove from the New Testament alone? Here is a partial list:

WAR
WARFARE
BATTLE
CONTEND
WRESTLE
RESIST
WITHSTAND
ENDURE
OCCUPY
FIGHT

ARMOUR
SWORD
ARM
ARMY
SOLDIER
WEAPONS
ENEMIES
ADVERSARY
OVERCOME
VICTORY

Most wars consist of a series of battles. A fierce battle is about to descend upon every pastor, teacher, apostle, evangelist and prophet sent from God.

George Barna, leader of The Barna Group, a respected research organization, has released the book, *Revolution*. In this book Barna reveals his prediction for the future of the church. If he is right, many God-called pastors will be eliminated from their pulpits as churches will be eliminated from the world's landscape.

Revolution calls this elimination of churches the "faith revolution that will redefine church—the most massive reshaping of the nation's faith community in more than a century."

This new faith revolution is heralded as becoming one of the most important spiritual movements of our age. Barna says he "will not be surprised if at some point this new revolution will become known as the Third Great Awakening in our nation's history."

He then defines this third awakening.

"This spiritual renaissance is very different from the prior two religious awakenings in America, but it may well become the most profound."

It is very different indeed.

The first two Awakenings filled the churches in America.

If this third "Awakening" takes place, it will empty them!

Barna states that the "Revolutionaries" will **leave** the church to **become** the church! They will leave the church "because they want more of God in their life but cannot get what they need from a local church!"

(Note: Does any preacher of God's Word tell his people that they get all they need in the church? Doesn't a true pastor encourage his congregation to seek God in a personal relationship, to read their Bibles daily, to pray daily, to witness daily, to give to the needy, to care for the sick, to help a neighbor, to raise their children in the fear of the Lord—to live out their Christianity every day at work and at home?)

This group of Revolutionaries will decide the best way to serve God in their neighborhoods will be to leave the church. Barna projects that by 2025 the local church will lose roughly half of its members. He claims "the church dropouts will be those who leave a local church **in order to increase their focus on faith** and to relate to God through different means."

He gives these examples of new approaches for these dropouts to relate to God:

Involvement in house churches.

Participation in marketplace ministries.

Use of the Internet to satisfy various faith-related needs or interests.

The development of unique and intense connections with other people who are deeply committed to their pursuit of God.

Barna predicts that "millions of committed born again Christians are **_choosing to advance their relationship with God_** by finding avenues of growth and service apart from a local church."

Pastor, please be aware of what is on our spiritual horizon.

Barna was asked if this meant that the "Revolution" could simply be a negative reaction to the local church.

Barna stated, "Most Revolutionaries go through predictable phases in their spiritual journey in which they initially become dissatisfied with their local church experience, then attempt to change things so their faith walk can be more fruitful. The result is that they undergo heightened frustration over their inability to introduce positive change, which leads them to drop out of the local church altogether, often in anger. But because **this entire adventure was instigated by their love for God and their desire to honor Him more fully**, they finally **transcend their frustration and anger** by creating a series of connections that allow them to stay close to God and other believers without involvement in a local church."

While this Revolution may be characterized by the pursuit of a stronger spiritual journey, Barna also points out that millions of people may abandon the entire faith community. "There is the danger of exposure to unbiblical or heretical teaching. There is the possibility of experiencing isolation from a true community of believers and the accountability and support that the church can provide."

Barna was also asked, "How do most Revolutionaries justify calling themselves devoted disciples of Christ while distancing themselves from a local church?"

His response was, "Many of them realize that someday they will stand before a holy God who will examine their devotion to Him. They could take *the safe and easy route of staying in a local church* and doing the expected programs and practices, but they also recognize that they will not be able to use a lackluster church experience as an excuse for a mediocre or unfulfilled spiritual life."

Barna also cites his own experience: *"Having been personally frustrated by the local church...."*

Yes, George Barna is one of many frustrated churchgoers and by his own admission is also now a member of the revolution.

The church is not perfect. Jesus made that clear when He addressed seven churches in the book of Revelation. He pointed out their weaknesses, sins and failures.

He also pointed out their strengths, faith and works.

Most revealing of all, Jesus addressed His messages to specific churches...not to an Internet surfer or a fisherman trolling the lake on a beautiful Sunday morning.

There are countless Christians who are throughout the entire world *being* the church!

Search for them, and you will find them running missions on city streets, holding Bible clubs in our public schools, evangelizing sinners in their neighborhoods, holding services in our parks, offering prayer in our hospitals, giving hope in our prisons, teaching children in their neighborhoods, singing the gospel in nursing homes, providing shelter for girls who do not choose an abortion, feeding the hungry in areas of devastation, taking the gospel to the mission fields.

When you find them, please ask them this question:

"Have you ever attended a church?"

It is doubtful that you will find even one involved in ministry who has never attended a church.

Yes, we may choose to label a massive church exodus a "Revolution."

And we may classify angry churchgoers as "Revolutionaries."

Remember that it was Jesus Christ who "gave some, apostles; and some, prophets; and some, evangelists; and some, pastors and teachers; for **the perfecting of the saints**...for **the work of the ministry.**" *Ephesians 4:11-12*

Beware of Satan's not so subtle plot against the Christian to abolish the church that Jesus founded and to remove the pastors that He sends to shepherd His flock! Satan attacks and uses every devious means possible to weaken, divide, and destroy Christ's appointed leaders who shepherd His flocks. If he defeats them, the sheep become prey for the wolves.

In a deathblow to the church, the destroyer could shut

the mouths of apostles, prophets, evangelists, teachers and pastors!

How many evangelists and apostles (missionaries) are sent out and supported by the church?

Prophets and teachers worked within the early church!

"Now there were *in the church* that was at Antioch certain *prophets and teachers*...." *Acts 13:1*

It is *Jesus* who gave leaders to the church!

This so-called Revolution is nothing more than a mutiny of rebellion against the church and its leaders!

Man is intelligent enough to know that nothing operates without leadership.

> Factories have foremen.
> Schools have superintendents.
> Classes have teachers.
> Cities have mayors.
> Police departments have chiefs.
> States have governors.
> Nations have presidents.
> Prisons have wardens.
> Offices have managers.
> Ships have captains.
> Bands have directors.
> Colleges have deans.
> Armies have generals.
> **_And churches have pastors._**

A mass exodus that Barna has predicted has already begun. It will surely result in mass confusion, simply because it is not written in the blueprint of God.

"Feed the flock of God which is among you," Peter wrote, **"taking the oversight** *(supervision; management; control)* thereof." *I Peter 5:2*

"Take heed therefore unto yourselves, and to all the flock, **over which the Holy Ghost hath made you overseers**, to feed the church of God, which He hath purchased with His own blood." *Acts 20:28*

Overseers are **foremen, caretakers, managers, and directors.**

Jesus gave pastors to the church.

The **Holy Ghost** appointed pastors as overseers.

This new revolution is nothing but the age-old rebellion against the Word of God. It began among mankind with Adam and Eve and continues still.

During the day that Paul penned the book of Hebrews, people were already leaving the church.

"**Not forsaking** the assembling of ourselves together, **as the manner (practice) of some is;** but exhorting one another: and so much the more, as ye see the day approaching." *Hebrews 10:25*

Those early dropouts complained as they left.

Paul tells us how they described his preaching: "For his letters, say they, are weighty and powerful; but his bodily presence is weak, and his speech contemptible *(horrible; lousy!)*." *II Corinthians 10:10*

Surely some complained that his sermons were too long.

"When he therefore was come up again, and had broken

116

bread, and eaten, and **talked a long while, even till break of day**, so he departed." *Acts 20:11*

There were probably many who grumbled about his preaching over their heads.

Peter said of Paul's writing, "...in which are some things hard to be understood." *II Peter 3:16*

Paul was upset that those who listened to his sermons could only digest milk, rather than the meat he longed to serve!

Paul tells us that the Church of Galatia "received me as an angel of God!"

"Ye would have plucked out your own eyes, and have given them to me!" he wrote.

The very next verse says, "Am I therefore become your enemy, because I tell you the truth?" *Galatians 4:14-16*

Apparently some no longer wanted to listen to Paul's sermons. There was simply too much truth in them!

Somehow through it all, we read: "And so were the **churches established** in the faith, and increased in number daily." *Acts 16:5*

If Barna's conclusions are accurate, the desire of many grumblers is to see the established churches eliminated once and for all, rather than to stay and seek to strengthen them.

Chapter 18

God Didn't Draft Cowards

Pastors, we have many more rough and tough battles to endure before we cross the finish line. If we were so naive as to think that the worst of our problems were behind us, we now know that the worst war against pastors is yet to come!

So...let us put on the whole armour of God, lift up the hands that hang down and go forth and **WIN THIS FINAL BATTLE!**

God didn't call COWARDS to be His soldiers!

Don't be AWOL from the field of battle! Don't be absent without leave!

Let us change AWOL to mean:

ALWAYS
WORKING FOR
OUR
LORD!

"Therefore, my beloved brethren, be ye steadfast, unmovable, **always abounding in the work of the Lord**, forasmuch as ye know that **your labour is not in vain in**

the Lord."

"They that sow in tears shall reap in joy. He that goeth forth and weepeth, bearing precious seed, shall doubtless come again with rejoicing, bringing his sheaves with him."

"Behold, we count them happy which endure!"

I Corinthians 15:58; Psalm 126:5-6; James 5:11

If You Are One

IF YOU ARE ONE...
who has made the path of a pastor a little bit harder
who has made his head drop a little bit lower
who has made his heart a little bit fainter
who has made his hands a little bit weaker
who has made his mind a little bit tenser
who has made his sleep a little bit lesser
who has made his smile a little bit duller
who has made his flock a little bit madder
who has made his wounds a little bit sorer
who has made his sea a little bit rougher
who has made his walk a little bit slower
who has made his burden a little bit heavier
and who has made his life a little bit sadder

COULD YOU SPEAK AN ENCOURAGING WORD...
to make his path a little bit smoother
to raise his head a little bit higher
to make his heart a little bit healthier
to make his hands a little bit stronger
to make his mind a little bit clearer

120

to make his sleep a little bit sweeter
to make his smile a little bit brighter
to make his flock a little bit gentler
to make his wounds heal a little bit better
to make his sea a little bit calmer
to make him walk a little bit faster
to make his load a little bit lighter
and to make his life a ***whole lot*** happier?

Can you hear the grief in Christ's words as He told of His prophets being killed and His messengers stoned?

"O Jerusalem, Jerusalem, which killest the prophets, and ***stonest them that are sent unto thee***; how often would I have gathered thy children together, as a hen doth gather her brood under her wings, and ***ye would not!***" *Luke 13:34*

Can you hear the contrasting joy in these words?

"Behold, how good and how pleasant it is for brethren to dwell together in unity!" *Psalm 133:3*

Can you see that Jesus wants us to receive His messengers?

"He that receiveth you receiveth me, and he that receiveth me receiveth him that sent me." *Matthew 10:40*

Can you hear the cry of God's heart in this passage?

"Now the God of patience and consolation grant you to be likeminded one toward another according to Christ Jesus:"

"That ye may **with one mind and one mouth glorify God**, even the Father of our Lord Jesus Christ."

"Wherefore receive ye one another, as Christ also received us to the glory of God."

"And be ye kind one to another, tenderhearted, forgiving one another, even as God for Christ's sake hath forgiven you." *Romans 15:5-7; Ephesians 4:32*

"So when they had dined, Jesus saith to Simon Peter, Simon, son of Jonas, lovest thou me more than these? He saith unto him, Yea, Lord; thou knowest that I love thee. He saith unto him, Feed my lambs. He saith to him again the second time, Simon, son of Jonas, lovest thou me? He saith unto him, Yea, Lord; thou knowest that I love thee. He saith unto him, Feed my sheep. He saith unto him the third time, Simon, son of Jonas, lovest thou me? Peter was grieved because he said unto him the third time, Lovest thou me? And he said unto him, Lord, thou knowest all things; thou knowest that I love thee. Jesus saith unto him, Feed my sheep." *John 21:15-17*

A Personal Invitation
to Pastors and Evangelists:

Foley, Alabama is situated between Mobile, Alabama and Pensacola, Florida. It is just 10 miles from the beautiful white sands of the Gulf of Mexico.

We have two completely furnished "Prophet's Chambers" on our church property. These are houses with full kitchens and comfortable living rooms. Both have two bedrooms. One has 2.5 baths. We offer these houses to pastors for a rest. There is no charge. For reservations, call Pastor Paul Wilde, (251) 949-7771.

"For we preach not ourselves, but Christ Jesus the Lord; and ourselves your servants for Jesus' sake."

II Corinthians 4:5

You may contact the author by writing or calling:

Paul and Carolyn Wilde
Telephone: (251) 949-7771
Email: pcwilde@gulftel.com

New Life In Christ Church
Pastor: Paul Wilde
102 E. Berry Avenue
Foley, Alabama 36535
Telephone: (251) 943-2225

Other Books by Carolyn Wilde

Torchbearers
Published by Whitaker House
ISBN: 0-88368-793-3

The thrill of victory coursed through his body, instantly expelling all weakness and pain. Dave was no longer an Olympic runner. He was now an Olympic Champion. Soon after he would be called to run the greatest race of all.

Fictional characters search through the centuries to find God's great torchbearers of the past. The 37 torchbearers you will meet in the pages of this book are real men, women and children who are part of our rich, but all too often forgotten, Christian heritage.

We've Come This Far by Faith
Published by River City Press, Inc.
ISBN: 0-9764232-4-3

As he lay injured in an ambulance beside his bleeding daughter, Paul Wilde made a promise to God. It was a life-changing commitment that led Paul, Carolyn and their eight children into an extraordinary, living-by-faith adventure.

Be challenged and inspired as you follow the faith journey of a family of ten who learned to trust God. The living and faithful God loves each of His children and cares about every single one of our needs!